Andre
Thank you
Focusing on effecting
change

The views expressed in this book are solely those of the author and not of any organization, governmental body, or other individual. Names, dates, and specific details of events, when necessary, have been altered for confidentiality purposes.

ISBN: 0997628103
ISBN-13: 978-0997628104

Cover design by Donald R. Guillory

Twitter: @donguillory
TheTokenBlackGuide@gmail.com
Facebook: Token Black Guide

This work is dedicated to my parents, Donald and Glenda for giving me the strength to always be myself, to my wife, Claudia, for her constant encouragement, to my daughter, Arya, whom I hope many of the issues and hardships faced by previous generations will not be revisited upon her, to all of my friends who kept me motivated, and to all of the "Tokens" in the world who carry the banner of their identity as a sword and a shield to battle the ignorance of the world.

The Token Black Guide

Donald R. Guillory

CONTENTS

Not everything that is faced can be changed.
But nothing can be changed until it is faced.

-James Baldwin

Despite everything, no one can dictate who you are to other people.

– Prince

Why I Write...

Growing up, my family held out hope that issues related to race and racism in America were continuously changing from the experiences that they had to deal with. Both products of the south, my parents wanted to keep the ugly realities of racism and race from me. They hoped that many of the problems and injustices that they had witnessed growing up would not be revisited upon me. Despite their wishes and concerns, I became more aware of the nuances and subtleties of racism as I grew older. Once my experience began, it was an education that would continue as I lived and traveled throughout the United States and abroad.

As hard as they tried through living in the "right" neighborhoods and putting me in the "good" schools, I would still bear witness to the bigotry, discrimination, social ills, and ignorance that they tried to protect me from. As we moved, due to my mother's military service, throughout the Midwest, West, and the South, I learned how the world that my parents and grandparents lived in still existed, however, the subtleties and the ignorance I experienced were merely subdued and muted by comparison.

By the time I entered college, I had become accustomed to being the "Token Black Guy." I always found myself becoming the "splash of color" in nearly every job, collegiate course or social interaction. I was consistently asked questions that people around me felt comfortable asking because they felt that I was somehow "safe" to talk to and a good source of information.

In America, we only discuss race when there is a major problem that has garnered the attention of the media or public officials. Our discussions often come in response to volatile and uncomfortable moments. They are hardly ever in a proactive manner, focused on dismantling the problems that led us to the moment we find ourselves. The discussions are highly reactive and lacking in substance or solutions. We often have this idea that we discuss race and the complexities of it. It's an illusion.

The topic of race and issues related to it have reached a point where we have so much confusion that people are beyond frustrated. We aren't having valid conversations of depth about where we stand and how situations affect us all because we are so hesitant to have these discussions. They put us on edge. They make us apprehensive. People avoid the issue of race out of the fear of potentially being thought of as racist due to their ignorance on matters or their unwillingness to confront the issues, at all. Some do not bother getting involved in discussions about race due to racism not having a direct impact on their lives. This is a disservice to true growth and closes possibilities for future change and progress on the racial frontier. We need to examine the institutional factors that contribute to racism continuing and further stymieing any progress. Race and the circumstances surrounding it are discussed in households of color on a daily basis, not just in times of crisis. It's a customary exchange between parent and child. This book serves to start a dialogue, contributing personal stories and historical examples of where people stand on some issues and why there is this "divide" over skin color."

My parents, to their credit, raised me to believe that my own skin color made me no better and no worse than anyone else. My mother taught me to treat others the way I wished to be treated. She desired a world in which we lived up to the values expressed in the Declaration of Independence that "All Men Are Created Equal" and the rights afforded to us in the Constitution are applied to all citizens whether they are white, black, brown, male, female, gay, straight, or any other identifying factor.

My mother was born the year that the Supreme Court's decision on *Brown v Board of Education* to desegregate schools was rendered, yet spent her life as witness to countless acts of racism, bigotry, and discrimination in rural Virginia. Growing up in the era of the Civil Rights movement, but experiencing the reality of the South, my mother wanted to break the cycle of violence. She witnessed countless acts of racism, bigotry, and discrimination growing up in rural Virginia. She watched the vestiges of Jim Crow Fall. She knew the pain that came with the early years of integration, as she sat at tables in the cafeteria, only for white students a table over to move because they didn't want to be seated near "Niggers." Over time, she thought that we had somehow surpassed this, but knew in her heart that there had only been minimal progress since she grew up in Virginia. That was never more evident than the night of the Trayvon Martin murder verdict.

It was a killing. It was another black face in America that had been erased and whose voice had been silenced. Trayvon was someone whose story would be altered due to ignorance and fear. He was labelled as a thug, a criminal, yet he was the victim. His character was assassinated in the court of public opinion with nearly the same cold approach that his assailant had when he took this young man's life. His story reminded me of the many instances of violence that had race as the subtext. There were so many questions involved in the killing and the way that the case was handled by the public and media. I was compelled to think about all of those times growing up that I could have fallen victim to the same violence that this young man had. I thought about the historical examples that I always looked to;

Emmett Till, Birmingham, Rosewood, Tulsa, Opelousas, and countless others. The case captivated so many people as we anxiously awaited the verdict.

My mother and I discussed the case and watched it unfold as she visited me in Arizona, but as the verdict came in, I observed her face as the heartache formed.

Not Guilty…

I sensed and feared what the verdict would be before it was announced and foolishly held on to the hope that Trayvon's killer would be convicted. It was a foregone conclusion. The living room was silent aside from the chattering of the talking panel on TV that was discussing the outcome of the case. I didn't know what to say or think at that moment. It felt as though time had stopped. My mother's voice cut through the silence and tension of that moment. Her words "our lives just don't matter" reverberated in my mind. "We just don't matter. No matter how much we do. How hard we work… What we sacrifice for this country… we don't matter. There is no one that can tell me any differently."

The façade that existed throughout her life, the one she built up in order to face the world each day, had been shattered. It seemed as though she felt somehow responsible for building that wall up and that she might have somehow failed her own children in trying to teach them that their self-worth mattered more than someone else's skewed perspective and worldview. As she rose, this proud, strong woman appeared so defeated by one example of the justice system. I reflected upon her words and came to the realization that countless incidents and occurrences had led to this point and sadly, they would continue.

I had watched my mother build herself up and work tirelessly in order to prove her worth and represent what diligence and integrity provided. My mother was reduced to the reality that all she had fought for in leaving Virginia to join the Army after high school, getting a college education, becoming a commissioned officer, serving her country with honor for nearly thirty years, and believing in many of the principles that many associate with American identity carried a little less weight. In fact, it seemed hollow.

I never witnessed the amount of struggle in my life that she had over the span of hers. I hadn't experienced a fraction of it. There was no comparison between our experiences. Her reaction was a mixture of disgust and disappointment in knowing that many of the fears that she had lived with throughout her life were being revisited in this case and in its verdict. Her entire identity was under assault. A woman in her late fifties who had given so much of herself to the United States and understood this to be her home. It was somewhere she should feel safe. What was her identity now? What was mine?

She was the mother of two sons and often warned us of the dangers that existed in the world, as any mother would, but never told us that we were different than anyone else or that we should expect to be treated as being worthy of less respect or dignity than anyone.

It would be years before I realized the value of these lessons. We were told to hold our heads up and look people in their eyes when speaking to them which many of her generation were discouraged to do. It was an issue that resulted in many black youth finding trouble or, more appropriately, trouble finding them when people felt "threatened by them."

I had to reexamine much of who I was and what had shaped me up to that point.

The next fall, my wife and I were awaiting the birth of our first child. The realization of many of the fears that I had from sitting down with my mother during the Trayvon Martin Murder trial crept back into my mind. I considered what challenges my child would face and the hope that I would have for people to treat her based on her merit and not on her skin tone, racial background, ethnicity, and heritage. It was a strange thought that in planning to become a father, one of the things I would have to consider whether or not my child would be treated like a human being. I slowly realized that this was the same mindset my parents found themselves in when preparing for my arrival and continues today for many families of color.

I had to face the reality that there is and have been a significant amount of people that never have to consider this aspect or put so much emphasis on these lessons and focus when raising their children. They never have to think about their child being followed around a store on the assumption that they were there to steal something. They don't have to consider that someone would tell them that their contributions mattered less or that they shouldn't take the advanced classes despite their grades. There is never the question that they will fit in when attending a predominantly white school or activities. They would be less likely to worry that their child may be verbally or physically assaulted because of the color of their skin, nor will they have to worry about their friends' parents refusing to have them sleep over in their house while many of their child's other friends are there frequently. I want my child to be judged for the content of her character and to be seen as more than an identity that someone else has assigned due to their deep-seated fears and bias. My child should be as free as any other child. Not talking about the issue will not spare her from any of these experiences.

Race has always been part of my life and existence, just as it has been part of the framework of American history and society. There were times that I tried to ignore it feeling as though it somehow didn't matter. It shouldn't matter in so many respects, but there are people who want it to matter so much as a way to degrade, discredit, or disparage me and other people of color. There is something faulty about who I am because of the level of melanin contained within my genetic coding. There is something wrong with my hair because of the way that it doesn't flow in the breeze. There is something wrong with trying to learn more about my history yet not having traditional avenues available due to much of the history being destroyed or distorted.

The problem with respect to the subject of race and racism is that we don't confront it. We collectively pass them on to the following generation, often resting on the laurels of the progress that we believe we have achieved in our own lifetimes or comparing circumstances with generations prior. We don't engage in any serious discussion to alleviate any of the social ills or address some of the problems driving them. We kid ourselves when as a society, we claim that we talk about race as a means to breaking down systemic conditions in order to bring about an end to disparity, strife, and inequality. Black parents give "the talk" well before there is any discussion about the "birds and the bees." Race comes up in black households throughout the nation in a way to remind ourselves and our children how the world works and how we can try to find our place in it. You are reminded of where you fit in the world. You are reminded of the cautions you should take. It is brought to your attention as to who you are and, more importantly, who you aren't. You are made aware of it in school, in the workplace, walking down the street, while shopping, at the gym, going out to eat, and even while traveling abroad. You are advised that you have to be twice as good in order to get half of the recognition. You are always in the spotlight and your actions are perpetually under a microscope. It is inescapable. I can't say the same for many of my white friends. In fact, when something involving race was witnessed, the response was typically "I didn't know things like that happened anymore" or worse, "you're overreacting."

There is a disconnect with black and white communities as to what is really going on. When minorities bring to light social injustices they are not simply whining or complaining about the unfairness that life brings. We are giving you a window into our realities. The dialogue needs to change and there is a need for us to all have these discussions. More importantly, it is imperative that there is some listening as part of these discussions and conversations instead of trying to make a case to downplay the realities and experiences. There needs to be a real substantive discussion about race and the experiences that people of color have in America. You need to understand before you can disagree.

The problem I have found when tackling these issues is that there are many who are willing to shut down the conversation before it ever picks up any steam by denying the conditions and circumstances that people deal with in order to avoid being uncomfortable or having their view of the world shattered. There are even instances in which people are completely dismissive because they do not want to engage in the discussion due to it not adhering to the narrative that they themselves have been accepting in their own mind and passing on to others for years. You need to understand before you can disagree.

The whole approach to the issue of racism is like Voldemort from the Harry Potter series. People ignore the possibility of it existing and avoid talking about it. When it is discussed, people claim that you are overreacting, imagining these circumstances or it is an isolated incident. They remain in this mindset unless they themselves see it in person or somehow perceive themselves as falling victim to it. Not having the conversation or addressing the reality for so many people allows the problems to persist. Confronting them allows for these problems to be seen. Seeing them allows for action to be taken against these injustices. The problem can be minimized and possibly eliminated. Communication is the first step and one that is well overdue. You need to understand before you can disagree.

This work and the experiences in it are all true. This is my offering to the conversation in order to help create a bit more understanding. Some of the moments are painful while others are humorous, but it is essential that stories and experiences like this are not buried so that we can collectively have a long overdue conversation about our situations and ensure that each generation is aware of some of the circumstances and experiences surrounding race so that they themselves can bring us to a point where a conversation will no longer be necessary. When that happens, we might just be able to finally talk to each other instead of needing to have a conversation.

We could all benefit from an examination and discussion of personal experiences within the "American Experience." This book and the occurrences shared within its pages will not save the world, nor will they end racism, but hopefully they will get a conversation started in your home, in your place of work, school, or just at least provide a glimpse of what it is like to be in someone else's shoes. The experiences are mine but are not exclusive to me. After years of finding myself in situations and circumstances, I went from being just another "Token Black Guy" to being the "Token Black Guide."

After reading the passages from this book, it is my hope that you have a better glimpse into at least one black person's experience with micro-aggressions, bigotry, discrimination, and misunderstandings. The experiences are mine, but these experiences are not limited solely to me. Hopefully, you'll come to understand and realize that there is more to fighting against racism and being on the side of diversity and inclusion than relying on your perceived personal references.

The Complexity of the 'Black Friend'

Token

Noun

A thing serving as a visible or tangible representation of a fact, quality, feeling, etc.

An item that can be exchanged for goods or services

Adjective

Done for the sake of appearances as a symbolic gesture

I can't remember the first time that I was referred to as a "Token." It has been brought to my attention so many times throughout my life that it has made me more conscious and apprehensive with regard to work, social gatherings, courses, workshops, and various activities. The designation of being the "Token," at times, I saw as an insult or even a curse. I thought that I was somehow an "Oreo" or "Uncle Tom" because of the propensity of finding myself as the only splash of color in situations. This status allowed me to see the world through different lenses during my life.

It is awkward to think about such a title as being the "Token Black" or the "Token" anything, for that matter. It is an identity that causes much confusion for the person assuming it and those who happen to unintentionally assign it to them. After all, why would anyone want to be one of the few and possibly only people of color or member of a marginalized group in their environment?

With America's long history of racial struggles, division, and misunderstandings, a "Token" at times can become the gateway into a culture for many of their non-black friends. It allows our friends to gain that glimpse into our world without having to go too deeply into it.

"Tokens" can be seen in all walks of life. Think about it. The one black anchor or weatherman on your local news, Franklin from *Peanuts,* every iteration of *Star Trek,* Lando Calrissian from *Star Wars,* Robin from *The Howard Stern Show,* and countless more African-Americans who helped to break down barriers of ignorance about what black identity and culture is.

We give our friends, coworkers, and strangers a glimpse into black perspectives, even if, occasionally, they are somewhat muted. We often are the focal point as to why friends and coworkers, because they have had a conversation or two with one of us, argue that they "are not racist."

We are the reason that they feel secure in their ability to make statements that are sometimes on the verge of being worthy for membership in the Aryan Nation. Being a "Token" or "safe" ensures a certain burden on us that we must bear for a variety of people and a variety of reasons. We have to balance being mascots and ambassadors. We find ourselves being the bridge between two worlds.

Racism is not some new phenomenon. Discovering who among your friends, family and coworkers is racist, bigoted or at least ignorant is getting more subdued and confusing as the years pass. Gone is the time when one could simply look at another individual and deem them as ignorant or intolerant solely in their affinity for yelling out the "N-Word" at any black person they cross paths with, wearing Klan robes and burning crosses on their neighbors' lawns, or making racist jokes amongst friends when any and all minorities are absent from their vicinity. With social progress, much of the language and norms that were more common for previous generations have become less present.

It is important to understand that "My best friend is black," or anything equivalent to this statement, does not translate into "I'm not racist." When you use this as your trump card to get you out of trouble in a dicey situation, you are doing nothing more than using your "friend" as a commodity rather than an actual friend. It cheapens the meaning of what a friend is and, devalues the entire relationship that you have. No one needs to use another individual to prove that they are not racist, sexist, homophobic, xenophobic, anti-Semitic, hateful or prejudiced to any group of people. We don't co-sign on your ignorance. If you aren't racist, you simply are not racist. There is no need to create a Supreme Court worthy statement of your case. We will, however, sit back and watch as you wedge your foot firmly into your own mouth.

If you truly want to break down these barriers and create a more inclusive society, don't silence our voices or dismiss and diminish our concerns. Have conversations with people about their experiences. As you do, listen. Don't focus on explaining your view of their perspective of the world and their experiences.

Someone's experience with cultural bias, ignorance, racism, bigotry, and discrimination is deeper than what you view their experiences to be or how they should see the world based on your perspective. Allow the discussions and subject matter to push you out of your comfort zone. You will learn, create a dialogue, and eventually transition from referring to your black friends as your "black friends."

It doesn't matter if you had a black friend in college, or if you are cool with the black guy or lady at work. It really doesn't matter if you dated a black guy in college or are married to one now. It doesn't even matter if you have mixed-race kids. Proximity does not give you access to the experience. If you are truly genuine in your efforts of including us and ensuring that racism and bigotry are confronted, there is a need to stop viewing us as pieces for a collection. We are not boxes to check off in order to achieve your personal racism immunity.

"CHANGE HAS COME?"

Everything felt different about the morning of November 4th, 2008. The night before felt as though there was a sense that history was going to be made and there was nothing that could stop it. It was inevitable.

Four years earlier, I was sitting with my girlfriend watching the Democratic National Convention when a young candidate for Senator from Chicago took to the podium and gave a rousing keynote speech. At its conclusion, I looked to her stating, "That guy is going to be President. Guaranteed. I'd put money on it."

When Senator Barack Obama announced his candidacy for the Presidency of the United States of America in 2007, I was not surprised, rather, I was quite pleased that he was throwing his hat into the ring. There were many who, even in the 21st century, could not see the possibility of an African-American running for and winning the highest public office in America. Much of the focus was on Hilary Clinton and it was a foregone conclusion that she was going to become the Democratic candidate and possibly win the Presidency.

The problem with American politics and the

political landscape was the image that many had towards African-Americans and African-American candidates. Black America and White America judged that candidates were either "not black enough" or "too black" for office based off of stereotypes and generalizations that had dug their way into people's perspectives and perceptions.

Senator Harry Reid stated what the problem was when he was quoted in the book "Game Change" by Mark Halperin and John Heilemann. According to his remarks, Obama was safe because "he was light-skinned and when he spoke he didn't carry any of the Negro dialect." This was turned into a series of stories through media outlets how Senator Reid was somehow racist by providing this commentary. The reality is that he was right. Senator Obama was not a caricature or stereotype that many could easily pick apart based off of his lack of style or political savvy. The issues then turned to guilt by association with respect to a Church where he was a member, accusations about him being a Muslim (which were nothing more than veiled ways to claim he was not "American"), and questions as to his citizenship in order to discredit him. There was nothing valid that could be used in order to criticize this candidate. He was constantly viewed as an "other."

The stories about him concerned issues that other candidates were not having to face nor were they being criticized about. Obama's patriotism was called into question because he did not wear a flag pin on his lapel for a period of time during the campaign. He was criticized again for not being "American" because he did not cover his heart when the national anthem was playing during an event. There were countless attempts to make this man who was trying to achieve his piece of the American dream and assert his identity according to what we collectively identify as "American."

During the campaign when the criticism hit its peak, he was forced to publicly defend himself and speak on race. This Presidential Candidate was not talking about his plans for the economy, defense, foreign policy, education, or any other concerns that were typical of a political candidate or even for his competitors. He was pushed into responding to a video of Reverend Jeremiah Wright, the Pastor of the Trinity United Church of Christ in Chicago where the Reverend gave a series of sermons that news outlets labeled as divisive and inflammatory. In his speech "A More Perfect Union," Senator Obama addressed the issues and laid out the reality of what many black men and women faced. He went so far as discussing how white relatives expressed their fear and distrust of black people. His speech voiced for many people what America's problems were. We were all too complacent or even afraid to discuss them. In his speech entitled "A More Perfect Union" he laid out all the issues that affected him throughout his life starting with the reason why he was even pushed to give the speech in the first place:

"In my first book, *Dreams From My Father,* I described the experience of my first service at Trinity:

> 'People began to shout, to rise from their seats and clap and cry out, a forceful wind carrying the reverend's voice up into the rafters....And in that single note – hope! – I heard something else; at the foot of that cross, inside the thousands of churches across the city, I imagined the stories of ordinary black people merging with the stories of David and Goliath, Moses and Pharaoh, the Christians in the lion's den, Ezekiel's field of dry bones. Those stories – of survival, and freedom, and hope – became our story, my story; the blood that had spilled was our blood, the tears our tears; until this black church, on this bright day, seemed once more a vessel carrying the story of a people into future generations and into a larger world. Our trials and triumphs became at once unique and universal, black and more than black; in chronicling our journey, the stories and songs gave us a means to reclaim memories that we didn't need to feel shame about...memories that all people might study and cherish – and with

which we could start to rebuild."

That has been my experience at Trinity. Like other predominantly black churches across the country, Trinity embodies the black community in its entirety – the doctor and the welfare mom, the model student and the former gang-banger. Like other black churches, Trinity's services are full of raucous laughter and sometimes bawdy humor. They are full of dancing, clapping, screaming and shouting that may seem jarring to the untrained ear. The church contains in full the kindness and cruelty, the fierce intelligence and the shocking ignorance, the struggles and successes, the love and yes, the bitterness and bias that make up the black experience in America.

The fact is that the comments that have been made and the issues that have surfaced over the last few weeks reflect the complexities of race in this country that we've never really worked through – a part of our union that we have yet to perfect. And if we walk away now, if we simply retreat into our respective corners, we will never be able to come together and solve challenges like health care, or education, or the need to find good jobs for every American.

Understanding this reality requires a

reminder of how we arrived at this point. As William Faulkner once wrote, "The past isn't dead and buried. In fact, it isn't even past." We do not need to recite here the history of racial injustice in this country. But we do need to remind ourselves that so many of the disparities that exist in the African-American community today can be directly traced to inequalities passed on from an earlier generation that suffered under the brutal legacy of slavery and Jim Crow.

Segregated schools were, and are, inferior schools; we still haven't fixed them, fifty years after Brown v. Board of Education, and the inferior education they provided, then and now, helps explain the pervasive achievement gap between today's black and white students.

Legalized discrimination – where blacks were prevented, often through violence, from owning property, or loans were not granted to African-American business owners, or black homeowners could not access FHA mortgages, or blacks were excluded from unions, or the police force, or fire departments – meant that black families could not amass any meaningful wealth to bequeath to future generations. That history helps explain the wealth and income gap between black and white, and the concentrated pockets of poverty that persists in so many of today's urban and rural communities.

A lack of economic opportunity among black men, and the shame and frustration that came from not being able to provide for one's family, contributed to the erosion of black families – a problem that welfare policies for many years may have worsened. And the lack of basic services in so many urban black neighborhoods – parks for kids to play in, police walking the beat, regular garbage pick-up and building code enforcement – all helped create a cycle of violence, blight and neglect that continue to haunt us.

This is the reality in which Reverend Wright and other African-Americans of his generation grew up. They came of age in the late fifties and early sixties, a time when segregation was still the law of the land and opportunity was systematically constricted. What's remarkable is not how many failed in the face of discrimination, but rather how many men and women overcame the odds; how many were able to make a way out of no way for those like me who would come after them.

But for all those who scratched and

clawed their way to get a piece of the American Dream, there were many who didn't make it – those who were ultimately defeated, in one way or another, by discrimination. That legacy of defeat was passed on to future generations – those young men and increasingly young women who we see standing on street corners or languishing in our prisons, without hope or prospects for the future. Even for those blacks who did make it, questions of race, and racism, continue to define their worldview in fundamental ways. For the men and women of Reverend Wright's generation, the memories of humiliation and doubt and fear have not gone away; nor has the anger and the bitterness of those years. That anger may not get expressed in public, in front of white co-workers or white friends. But it does find voice in the barbershop or around the kitchen table. At times, that anger is exploited by politicians, to gin up votes along racial lines, or to make up for a politician's own failings.

In fact, a similar anger exists within segments of the white community. Most working- and middle-class white Americans don't feel that they have been particularly privileged by their race. Their experience is the immigrant experience – as far as they're concerned, no one's handed them anything, they've built it from scratch. They've worked hard all their lives, many times only to see their jobs shipped overseas or their pension dumped after a lifetime of labor. They are anxious about their futures, and feel their dreams slipping away; in an era of stagnant wages and global competition, opportunity comes to be seen as a zero-sum game, in which your dreams come at my expense. So when they are told to bus their children to a school across town; when they hear that an African American is getting an advantage in landing a good job or a spot in a good college because of an injustice that they themselves never committed; when they're told that their fears about crime in urban neighborhoods are somehow prejudiced, resentment builds over time.

Like the anger within the black community, these resentments aren't always expressed in polite company. But they have helped shape the political landscape for at least a generation. Anger over welfare and affirmative action helped forge the Reagan Coalition. Politicians routinely exploited fears of crime for their own electoral ends. Talk show hosts and conservative commentators built entire careers unmasking bogus claims of racism

> while dismissing legitimate discussions of racial injustice and inequality as mere political correctness or reverse racism.
>
> Just as black anger often proved counterproductive, so have these white resentments distracted attention from the real culprits of the middle-class squeeze – a corporate culture rife with inside dealing, questionable accounting practices, and short-term greed; a Washington dominated by lobbyists and special interests; economic policies that favor the few over the many. And yet, to wish away the resentments of white Americans, to label them as misguided or even racist, without recognizing they are grounded in legitimate concerns – this too widens the racial divide, and blocks the path to understanding. (Obama 2008)

In his analysis and the delivery of that speech, he opened the conversation with mainstream America as to what the reality was for millions of African-Americans throughout the nation. He related the struggles that many of us had experienced. Until this moment, no one had the opportunity to articulate this problem with a forum or position of this magnitude without it being related to the Civil Rights Movement.

America was more than overdue for someone of

his background and on this level of public platform to speak to a national audience about matters of race and class in order to address these issues. This opportunity was delivered to him and provided a way for all of us, despite the ethnic, racial, religious, and class differences to have a substantive conversation about race and the issues inherent to it for the first time since the Civil Rights movement. The problem is that many people felt as though many of those issues and accomplishments of the Civil Rights movement were settled and equality under the law translated into equality as a reality. This was not the case and it was proven in that election.

After the speech, consultants, pundits, politicians, public officials, and journalists evaluated the weight of what Senator Obama said. People who witnessed the speech discussed the ideas and issues brought up. Whether they were Democrat or Republican, Black or White, much of the response was positive and addressed the issues that he raised. There were questions as to where we should collectively go from that point on. People from all walks of life evaluated the importance, reach, appropriateness, and value of Senator Obama's speech. It was clear: it had to be done and his words needed to be said, not just in response to the criticisms of his preacher, but to bring to light many of the simmering issues that America faced and continues to face. People who had been critical of Senator Obama's handling of the Reverend Wright incident thus far, saw him differently. When discussing his speech, many remarked that Obama was the only person in the country who could have given a speech like that. No one else, they argued, black or white could have given it with the same purpose and effect. He was the right person in the right place at the right time. His speech for many, was honest and personal. It drove home the issues and made them establish a connection to all those who were willing to listen to what he had to say.

For the first time, it seemed as though we were going to have a real conversation about race and about the circumstances involved with it. There were many prominent public figures of all political ideologies who came forward praising the candidate's speech. Republicans and Democrats alike saw this as a true moment in which there could be some real change made with respect to how we discussed race and issues related to it. The optimism was short lived.

When elected that Fall, many saw this moment as marking some sort of "post-racial" moment in America. We held a collective breath and hoped that social transformation would take place within our nation allowing all of us to reach across racial, cultural, class, religious, gender, and whatever barriers divided us. The reality was that it led us into a world where post-racial came to mean the more bigoted of us found shelter and solace in the convenience of having a black president. They could say blatantly racist or offensive things and it wasn't them being racist, it was just you being overly sensitive. They could offer up that the world around them was one in which racism did not exist because America had elected a black man as president, therefore racism was over. They no longer had to rely on that one black friend that they kept tucked away in their back pocket for special occasions as some sort of racism insurance policy for them. Their "friendships" could serve as some sort of deductible to protect them from allegations of bigotry and racism. Racism was now over because Obama was elected. Every Token Black Friend was now without a home. Some of us had to regroup and contemplate our next move with respect to racial navigations. For closeted bigots, the mentality was "I can say or do something blatantly racist or bigoted and use the excuse that racism is over because the President is black. If you call me on it, you're just being too PC, besides, I still can't say the N-Word!"

We had so much opportunity to see this in action during his presidency and one of the first incidents occurred when a close friend, celebrated professor, scholar, author, and filmmaker, Dr. Henry Louis Gates was arrested in 2009. The incident drew national attention because of who Dr. Gates is, as well as the circumstances surrounding the arrest. Dr. Gates had arrived home from a trip abroad and when he had trouble getting his door open, asked his cab driver for assistance. Minutes later, the police arrived to question Dr. Gates as to why he was there. Even after proving that this was his residence and having shown his identification, he was arrested for refusing to step outside of the home. This should outrage anyone and when placed in his shoes, one should understand his frustration and question the purpose of why one is being treated like this in their own home even after proving that it is theirs.

There was no valid reason that he could imagine for the police to stay once he proved who he was and why he was there. The officer informed him that he was there to investigate a possible robbery and that his neighbor called the police to report that two black men had broken into the house. There were at least two issues at play here that many had trouble with, including myself. The neighbor's suspicions of these "black men" entering the house and the police officer's persistence to follow through with an investigation when there was no need to investigate a crime that had not been committed. When approached about the incident, the President, being a friend and colleague of Dr. Gates remarked that the Police had "acted stupidly" in their handling of the situation and arrest of the professor. Quickly, race became the primary issue. With the President's relationship with Dr. Gates, the topic turned to how he must somehow be divisive considering that the officer was white and his friend, whom he took up for, was black. The President would ultimately be forced into the role of a peacemaker in throwing the "Beer Summit" at the White House inviting both Dr. Gates and Sgt. James Crowley in order to heal the wounds, achieve a sense of closure over the incident, and discuss issues related to racial profiling that persist throughout the nation.

More incidents would occur over his presidency, but it was the Trayvon Martin case that really brought the President's role as a father and his experience as a young black male into play. When discussing this case with the press, as he discussed many issues, he made a statement that many people could and should have been able to identify with or understand his message:

> You know, when Trayvon Martin was first shot I said that this could have been my son. Another way of saying that is Trayvon Martin could have been me 35 years ago. And when you think about why, in the African American community at least, there's a lot of pain around what happened here, I think it's important to recognize that the African American community is looking at this issue through a set of experiences and a history that doesn't go away.

> There are very few African American men in this country who haven't had the experience of being followed when they were shopping in a department store. That includes me. There are very few African American men who haven't had the experience of walking across the street and hearing the locks click on the doors of cars. That happens to me -- at least before I was a senator. There are very few African Americans who haven't had the experience of getting on an elevator and a woman clutching her purse nervously and holding her breath until she had a chance to get off. That happens often. (Obama 2013)

He personalized the moment. He explained the historical weight and its legacy. It was such a simple, straight-forward outlook with respect to the incident. His view was truthful, honest, and genuine just as it was when he delivered his "More Perfect Union" speech. It was a view that every American parent held when this happened and internalized, but it was his position and identity for some people that turned it into an issue based solely on race. The President pointed out what the issue was and that it needed to be addressed. Not doing so would be a failure on the part of his office to recognize these inconsistencies with policies, practices and social norms. To put it simply, the President didn't stop being black when he took the oath of office. His identity didn't change. The baggage and learning experience inherent with being who he is did not magically become nonexistent once he crossed the threshold of the Oval Office. None of the circumstances of his identity nor experiences had been removed from his memory. The complexities when situations like this arise is that he and minority members of Congress of color have to communicate to their peers what their experiences are like. It is hard for someone to contemplate the President of the United States at one time being followed around a store because he "looks suspicious," not being able to get a cab due to the fear tied to the hue of his skin, the idea that an individual is thought of as less qualified for a job or less intelligent than his peers, that he is more likely to be found in a den of crime than as a productive member of society.

As President, one of the unofficial roles is "consoler-in-chief." In performing this duty, he internalized the pain that this family was going through as he has expressed for many families when questioned about their loss. He did not make it about race despite the reality of racial elements and issues of bigotry surrounding this case, investigation, and media coverage. For many, it seemed as though the President was injecting race into the events or trying to be divisive on the issue by tapping into some long held, deep seated hatred in order to score political points. This was not the case. He simply recognized and rationalized what many of us were thinking in our homes whenever we saw an act of violence perpetrated on the news or on our streets: "That could have been me. That could have been someone I loved." His tone, grief, and sentiment on the circumstances were as deep as those expressed in his response to the Sandy Hook murders. The unfortunate reality is that when there was personal identification with a black child, he was somehow racially motivated.

President Obama's race is both his gift and his curse given his public position. He has the ability to bring his voice to many of the concerns and issues that people of color uniquely face. His position affords him the opportunity to bring these issues to the attention of mainstream America from a perspective and position that previous Presidents had not been able to. They may have had friends or family members of color, but there is no substitute or equivalent for having that life experience and living in that skin.

The burden that he bears is that in the times that he does voice the concerns for people of color, there are those who feel he is being divisive or trying to inject race into a conversation. Unfortunately for these people, they are not facing the reality that has existed for generations; race has been the burden of this nation since before its founding. It is one that we have yet to come to terms with and having a President who is black does not negate that history or make those issues disappear.

The election of Barack Obama ensured that we need to continue this dialogue and make sure that there is even more opportunity for people and more voices for those who cannot speak up.

You're one of the 'Good Ones'

"You're one of the Good ones" is not a compliment. It's not even close. When you feel this phrase coming out of your throat and passing through your teeth, try very hard to cut it off before you wind up ending a good relationship.

I can't remember the first time I was told this nor the last, but I can remember the most profound moment. I was a senior in high school taking journalism as my elective when the course sponsor, Mrs. C., pulled me aside as I was walking down the hall from the lab. She looked a little frustrated and bothered. She and I butted heads from time to time about articles that appeared, timelines, or even my sense of humor, but none of these were the case on this occasion.

As she passed me in the hall one afternoon, she grabbed my arm to get my attention and stated, "You know… I have to tell you… you… you're one of the good ones."

I first thought it was complimentary and intended to reflect upon my work ethic. Perhaps it was in reference to my grades, attitude, or how I carried myself. I even considered that it may have been in comparison to my generation. Generation X had been labeled the "overlooked generation," the "neglected middle child," "slackers," and those with little to no ambition or prospects. We were a generation that was deemed to be filled with potential, but lacked the will and drive. Any number of things would have been acceptable. The smile on my face, in response to what seemed to be a note of praise at the time, quickly soured into a sullen, stagnant grimace due to her line of explanation and logic.

"Day after day, I feel that my black students are just wasting their time here. Some days I just want to tell them 'Why don't you just drop out and go on welfare.'" She didn't say that she wanted to push her students to work harder. She didn't say that she wanted to convince her students that an education was worth the effort; that they should stay in school and perhaps pursue a college education. She didn't even mention the career paths that were open to these kids once they were to leave those hallways. She went for the dead end. Drop out. Welfare. She made her feelings crystal clear. She didn't care about "them." They were the "other." They were unwelcome. They were taking up space. It would be so much more convenient and suitable for them to be expurgated.

Up to that point, I had been willing to accept a compliment from her. Praise from any teacher can feel significant because someone in authority recognizes your accomplishments; but her compliments had transformed from admiration of my abilities, talents and ambitions into the denigration of an entire race.

I no longer felt accomplished in what I had done for myself with my studies, grades and accolades. It was as though she saw me as some mascot, or racial experiment that could be paraded around and lauded over. In her twisted mind the black students that she taught were only her burden until they had reached the age to where they could learn how to fill out a state assistance form. I was the exception to the rule according to her and not the norm. It was expected from day one for black students who entered the doors of this school to go on welfare, become drug-addicted, and not get an education. School was just a way station between their homes and a future in the projects. Their attendance in school was a formality. I was "exceptional" because I surpassed some imaginary racial limitations imposed by this teacher's perceptions and perspectives with respect to blackness and black identity. She and countless other teachers thought in this manner. As a result, students are not presented with the opportunity to think about the potential they possess or strive further. Subsequently, these educators only see the dead ends they have created by not affording their students the chance to reach their own potential. These educators do not understand that these students are no different than the students they praise and give second, third, and fourth chances to on a regular basis. They just see them differently because of their surface and refuse to see their own hand in creating the dead ends that they despise so much.

"I don't see color."

This is another one of those well-meaning statements that makes me cringe. It isn't stating that the person is not opposed to racism, even though it is implied, but what it ends up meaning is that instead of accepting the concept of someone's identity, race, ethnicity, and culture, the individual then turns it into an issue where they are trying to define the person as something in which they are comfortable with. This defeats the purpose in trying to face up to the issues and circumstances surrounding race, ethnicity, culture, and identity. It dilutes the dialogue. Race and ethnicity are matters that people deal with and are affected by on a daily basis. Choosing to see someone according to your own definition ignores the reality that many of these people live in. This results in people consistently not confronting any of the problems surrounding race, racism, social inequality, prejudice, or discrimination.

When you "don't see color" you fail to acknowledge a portion of me that has helped to shape my history and identity. You are saying that this history doesn't matter nor should it be considered. The color of my skin and race do not solely define me, but they do play a vital role in who I am. It leads to the likelihood that you will not recognize the injustices that people of color suffer. Colorblindness makes one blind and deaf to inequality, prejudice, and discrimination. It renders you as indifferent and uninterested in actually pushing for change. You are not colorblind; you are actively choosing to ignore reality.

"I don't see color" means nothing more to me than "I don't see you, your history, circumstances, or existence. So, there is no way I could understand what obstacles that you face. But saying this simple phrase makes me feel comfortable in thinking that I have reassured you through an empty platitude that I am not racist."

Your blindness to my exterior reflects the blindness that you have with reality. Your ability to not see my color prolongs your inability to see circumstances and reality that I encounter. It leads to the excuses that people make or try to find with any and every encounter that involves race. If I tell you that the police pulled me over or I'm being followed around the store, you are quick to argue that I must have done something to warrant it. There is something about my behavior or conduct that was perfectly good rationale for being stopped, accosted, and disturbed. You are willing to accept any reason other than the possibility that the only reason I was a recipient of this targeting may be linked to my skin. It's not about my music, sagging jeans, or my "attitude." It might just be that thing that you are failing or refusing to see. My ability and willingness to talk about it is not casting blame on you. I just want you to listen to the circumstances and issues in order to empathize with what many people face each day.

See my color. Value it. Learn from it. Don't judge me by it and don't become blind to it. When you see me, you might be able to see the conditions that many people just like me face.

"You're not *really* black"

These words can end a relationship or start an altercation. What you are really saying is that you have long-held, deep-rooted stereotypes and generalizations that you hold true and that my ability to not conform to or my ability to surpass those generalizations somehow does not fit your definition of blackness or black identity. What has really occurred is that I changed your perception of what a black person is and you are uncomfortable giving up those stereotypes because it might, deep down, mean that you are somehow racist and that makes you uncomfortable. Maybe you can adjust your thinking and see me as an individual and not a preconceived identity that must fit into a box in order for you to feel comfortable. It demeans individual identity. Additionally, it becomes an issue of judgment of my race and culture based upon what you think I should conform to.

Continuing this idea of what parameters of "Blackness" falls into does nothing more than place limitations on us. It makes those of us who do not conform seem somehow less worthy of this skin and pushes us to being anomalies and outliers when our characteristics, attitudes, actions, activities, and appearance are more common than you can imagine. We are not unicorns.

Saying and believing statements like "you're not really black," is an attempt to ridicule and delegitimize someone's skin, race, history and personal experiences. You want them to make you comfortable with their "blackness" and ignore what makes this individual comfortable in their own skin because you don't feel that it is authentic enough. You want us to follow the rules that you set on who and what we are. Black people, and all other ethnicities, for that matter, are not created with recipes. You can't add a dash of this or an ounce of that in order to make someone who is "genuinely Black" according to the formula that you were taught your whole life would result in a "Negro."

Our tastes and styles are quite varied. Not all of us listen to Hip-Hop or went to HBCUs. Most of us didn't grow up in the "ghetto." Some of us grew up in the suburbs with a handful of our own black friends whom we competed with about our authenticity. Some of us love Anime, Country music, and Metal. Some of us have never had greens. Some of us are Vegans. Some of us put salt on our grits while others apply sugar. There are some of us who have never even tasted them. Some of us grew up with English as our second language. Many of us can't play sports if our lives depended on it. Some of us have no rhythm whatsoever and avoid the dance floor at all costs. Some of us are Republicans. Some of us are even Atheists.

We are a diverse people and community. There is much more to us than the generalizations that have been built up for years and have determined how groups and individuals that have had limited contact with us have come to define us. We need to be in a "box" for others so they can be comfortable in identifying us as though we were subject to some sociological or anthropological study. Any deviation means that they were wrong and now they don't know how to classify us so we must not really "be black."

We are products of our environments, families, and histories, just as anyone else. Our identities are not products meant for your consumption nor are they meant to be defined, evaluated, or rejected by you. Blackness is not a trend, fad, or fetish. It is not about boxes that can be checked off or characteristics to adhere to in order to validate someone's identity. Listening to certain music, dressing in particular style, speaking in a way that incorporates African-American Vernacular English (AAVE), or any other accepted generalization and oversimplification does not determine blackness. What's more ridiculous is that someone who looks at the experience of black people, cherry pick the "cool" parts in order to grade other black people on whether or not they qualify to live in their own skin. Statements like "You're not really Black," or "I'm Blacker than you" implies that my identity deserves your scrutiny.

Somehow my identity is not valid but your ignorance and adherence to stereotypes is.

Invisible Man

There were 10 of us sitting around the large conference table. Interaction was made simple by the intimacy of the course. We were discussing life experiences and the way that money and perspectives of money and material goods change over generations. The discussion and dialogue was intriguing. The conversation was flowing so well that no one seemed to notice that one of the other graduate students was missing. With it being a small enrollment, we tended to notice when someone was absent, considering that it changed the dynamics greatly.

Brent, one of the other students assembled in this room chimed in, "I really wish that Renee were here. I would love to get her experience and perspective as an African-American. I really am curious as to how a black person would have read this information and be able to hear how it is applied. Her insight as an African-American would be great for this type of discussion."

Hello???

Brent was sitting right next to me in our Graduate Seminar. Literally right next to me. If he had stretched out his arms he would have hit me in my chest.

Does this dude really not see me?

My friend Paulette who was sitting directly across from me tried to contain her laughter as she noticed me smirking in response to the curiosity. I shrugged and held in a chuckle of my own before placing my index finger over my lips in order to indicate that she should not reveal our "secret" to Brent. He was none the wiser.

The session came to a close not too long after this awkward moment. Upon leaving the room, I headed back to my desk in the Graduate Assistants' office to drop off my notes and found Renee sitting at her computer.

"Renee, I thought you weren't here today."

"I had some research to finish and this was the only time I could get anything done. Was Dr. R looking for me?"

"Nope, but you were sorely missed," I chuckled.

"What do you mean? What's so funny?"

I proceeded to tell her of the moment that has just taken place. She let out a hearty laugh and turned to me.

"He really said all that?"

"Yup. Apparently, I am blessed with the superpower of invisibility."

"That's exactly what I've been telling you. They keep forgetting that you are black. You just seem so non-threatening. Either that or they think I'm 'blacker' than you. What did he expect from me anyway? Did he think I was going to have some stories about being downtrodden and growing up in the projects dodging drug dealers, prostitutes, and gang violence on my way to school? I'm from the suburbs just like you." She continued laughing.

We All Look Alike

I have lost track of how many times someone I have worked with, taught, run into in public, or the friend of a friend stated how much I looked like another black person or celebrity. Some were flattering and others were, well, unsettling.

When looking at the list that these people compiled for me, I thought to myself, does the stereotype and belief actually exist that people think that we all look alike actually hold weight? As I looked at and compared all of the images of these men, I knew better than to think that all of them looked alike. I hardly even noticed a resemblance between any of them and myself aside from skin tone. I had a blind date tell me that I looked like Shemar Moore (I'll take it). A random stranger remarked Anthony Anderson. Classmates would state Malcolm X. Ever since *Star Trek: The Next Generation* debuted people notified me of my resemblance to Michael Dorn. Each Comic-Con I attend someone is bound to run after me in order to get a photo or autograph only to be sorely disappointed when I fully turn around.

My high school students thought I looked like Rondell Sheridan from *That's So Raven,* Ice Cube, Ice-T, and Uncle Phil from *The Fresh Prince of Bel-Air*. A stranger stopped me in the men's room, thus breaking guy code, to tell me I looked like Jordan Peele from the television show, *Key and Peele.* It has been an inexhaustible, never-ending list of names and faces.

I've taken a long hard look at each of these guys and never saw the resemblance, similarities, or commonalities. Well, there's one.

"American" Me

I had moved to Georgia in 1989 when the Army relocated my mother and, by default my brother and me, outside of Atlanta. After serving the last few years of her commitment, the decision to remain in the Army hinged on her next assignment. It was between Hawaii and Germany. If it was Hawaii, she was going to stay in. If it was Germany, she would not sign onto a new contract. The paperwork came back: Germany. We would now set up shop in the South. The South wasn't anything new to me considering that my father's family has been in Louisiana since before it was part of the United States. My mother's side were all in Virginia. Considering the location of Georgia, this would be ideal in ensuring that there was still a connection to both sides of the family. I could go and visit my father during breaks or holidays and continue to spend Summers in Virginia with my cousins.

By the time I graduated from high school I had been accepted to Emory, Mercer, Georgia Tech, the University of Georgia, a few out of state schools, and one in-state school that I had never heard of: Georgia Southern. Georgia Southern was located in a town I had never heard of, but sounded as though it was frozen in time: Statesboro. It was a small town whose population doubled during the academic year with the influx of students.

I had received the packet in the mail one day along with a VHS "welcome to campus" tape. Georgia Southern was all I could afford with the limited financial aid available to me at the time and the savings that I had accumulated from work. I had to be practical. This school would have to do, at least for the time being. For my undergrad years, I always kept my eyes on the horizon and thought about a career path that would take me out of the South.

I quickly learned that the town in which this college was located had not progressed much from the 1950s and in some respects, the 1850s. There were Confederate memorials and an air of hostility that would hold this town to its less than progressive ways. There was a section of town known as "black bottom" that had lines of shotgun shacks and was the picture of abject poverty. Each day, I was reminded of how far we have still not progressed.

While attending school, I had a variety of jobs on campus and off. Nearing my Junior year of college, I was offered a pretty well-paying job at the local mall. It offered decent hours and afforded me with the ability to continue my education and not derail my future plans.

After a year, I had been promoted to a managerial position with the store. It came with more responsibility and a little more autonomy. During the week, it was not too uncommon for me to be the only employee in the store. Many of these days saw sales slow to a trickle where I often had no more than one or two people cross the threshold over the course of 3-4 hours.

When it is a slow work day, for most of us, all we can really expect is for time to slow down and our sensitivity to the ticking clock increase exponentially. The highlights of our day, especially when working in retail is that someone will come in, engage in conversation, and eventually make a purchase in order to give us a respite from the monotony.

I stood behind the register after checking the shelves and displays for a fourth time when two elderly southern white women walked in needing my assistance. We walked around the store as I assisted them with their shopping needs. I wasn't prepared for the remainder of our interaction. When it came time to check out, reality set in. The two women divided up their items in order to pay separately. As one of the ladies was paying for her items, her friend looked me over.

"Excuse me, but are you American?" asked one of the women in her syrupy southern drawl.

American?

I was taken aback, but responded "Yes, ma'am." I've gotten that from time to time living in Georgia. Often it was because of my "articulated speech," skin tone, and mannerisms. I wasn't quite sure where this was heading, but I knew it wasn't good. Something about me, at least to her, seemed foreign, different. I began to feel as though this question had miles of baggage behind it and I was apprehensive as to engaging her query. Her question and the tone in which it was asked made me think about being American and the idea of not fitting into what "American" means. It is something I have thought about throughout my life. I am an American citizen. I reside within the borders of the United States, but am I truly American? Images that resemble me and hold my features are not actively promoted throughout the nation or abroad in order to demonstrate that I am included in the definition and someone who possesses the attributes of what it means to be an American. I am American, but I am not certain that I am "an American." For some reason, I looked and seemed foreign to many people in the south. There was always something to them that made them feel as though I was an "other."

"You remind me of our friend Paul, she continued, "He's from one of them countries."

One of them countries?

My suspicions had been confirmed. I looked like

an "other." There was no way to escape this situation. I had concluded the transaction with her friend, who didn't take a role in our conversation, and had yet to process her purchases. I longed for this uncomfortable interaction to come to a conclusion.

I continued to contemplate her question. What exactly is "American?" Are there rules? Is there a look? What defines "Americanness?" More importantly, what excludes you? To this woman, my identity was already called into question. There is much hidden behind her words. It wasn't simply about whether or not she wanted to know about my nationality. What purpose was there other than trying to establish as to whether or not I was an "other?" To her, I looked and sounded "different."

I was not American or American enough, in her eyes. There was something flawed about my identity. I did not meet the definition of who or what an American should be. She had to draw some distinction between the two of us, or try to find some kinship. It was about differentiation between the two of us. It was not a serious inquiry or one that was based on curiosity, it was to create a distinction. I was an "other."

I thought to myself that there could be no positive ending to this situation. As she handed me her money to pay for her items. she started to stumble through a collection of third-world and imaginary nations in her attempt to inform me of the country that her friend and I might share.

"Ma… ma…"

"Malawi?" I guessed.

"No."

"Papa something."

"Papua New Guinea?"

I found a sense of pride that many of the countries I had learned in my history and geography courses in high school were now coming into use.

"No."

"Palau? No, that's not it," she thought aloud.

"Samoa?" I offered.

"Paul's from Guam," her friend finally interjected.

"You're right! Guam! Guam!" She exclaimed as though she had won a prize.

"Paul's from Guam! I can't believe I forgot that. He's always getting mistaken for a Nigra!"

My jaw dropped on the floor and my blood began to boil at the level of ignorance that this lady expressed. I couldn't believe that I had been put in this position of ignorance. I had heard this term before in films, television shows, and even read it in books before, but I had never heard it in person. I was a "Nigra;" a term and identification that demonstrated her ignorance, prejudice, and need to differentiate the two of us.

I was on the periphery of what an American is. My status was steps below hers based on the way that she asked me about my identity and immediately turned to how I resembled a friend who was "from one of them countries." I looked at both women and thanked them for their purchases.

As they walked out, I thought about all of the stupid incidents that had happened growing up when someone would use race against me. I thought about how the black students made me feel as though I didn't fit in because I wasn't black enough. I thought about the girls I would ask out in high school who couldn't go out with me because their parents didn't approve of their daughter dating a black kid. I thought about how I always felt alone in my honors classes by being the only black student. I recalled the interactions I had where people thought that I "sounded white." I thought of so many moments in which the misconceptions and generalizations on race dictated behavior

I watched as they completely exited the store and turned the corner out of my view. It was then that all feeling about their indiscretion passed and I thought more about how stupid it was for people to hold onto feelings and beliefs of others being inferior to them, due to their race, ethnicity, or nationality.

I started to laugh. I had no anger about it, just laughter. It was a moment in which I could not express anger. I felt compelled to look past her ignorance. It was a moment in which the sheer audacity of her statement shocked me in a way that there was no way to respond other than laughter. There are some moments of racial ignorance where you can't expend the energy to get angry about the issue. I just stood there alone in the store and laughed.

"Friendly" Skies

I hate flying. I detest nearly everything about air travel. The cramped quarters. The invasion of personal space. The feeling as though the walls are caving in around you and the idea of being in the air for hours under someone else's control always made me anxious… plus there was my fear of heights. As a result, I always avoided flying.

When I pursued my undergraduate degree in International Studies, I came to grips with the idea that studying foreign cultures and history would at some time require me to travel abroad. Reading and researching about the people and history of Cuba, Chile, Brazil, France, England, and the diversity throughout the continent of Africa would not be enough to appreciate what traveling there in person would offer. I would need to visit these places, speak to the people, see the historic sites and absorb the culture and history in order to truly make my degree and my studies worthwhile. I had traveled to France in January of 2003 to get the first "bugs" out of my system and get over the fear of flying. That voyage opened my eyes to the possibilities that would further await me in my cultural travels, explorations, and endeavors. Upon my second venture overseas in 2004, I was exposed to how I was part of the American framework and yet still not.

When I began my graduate studies, I worked with one of my professors on several projects, one of which involved studying the relationships between the United States and Great Britain during the Civil War. As part of this research, I was afforded the ability to complete some of my research in London making use of the Public Records Office and the British Library. It was a remarkable opportunity that I could not pass up.

That May, as the semester came to an end, I had my housing and travel plans arranged and awaited my chance to spend the next two and a half weeks in archives, hostels, museums, historic sites and enjoying my break from Southeast Georgia.

Hartsfield Airport was as busy as it normally is and with this being just the second flight in my adult life, I made sure to get to the airport as early as possible. I checked and rechecked everything that I had in order to make sure that there was nothing I hadn't missed and nothing that I would need to buy just before boarding the plane. The flight attendants made their notices from the gate and it was time to make my way to London aboard this British Airways flight.

As I boarded the plane, I waited for other travelers to find their seats. When the opportunity came, I headed for mine. 30E, a middle seat. Out of habit and comfort, I never pick middle seats, but with this trip, I had little choice. When I purchased the ticket and had the opportunity to choose my seat, the only option provided for me was a seat in between two others.

With my carry-on stowed and my reading material and CD player out, I prepared for takeoff. An older gentleman approached my row. I rose to let him into his seat by the window and he gave me a puzzled look.

Almost as if we had some sort of cosmic connection, he asked me, "Are you sure you are in the right seat?" At that moment, I thought to myself *of course I was in the right seat... I bought the ticket... Don't you see me sitting here?* I bit my tongue and responded, " Why yes, sir. That's what it says on my ticket."

He didn't seem too pleased, either at my response or that I was sitting next to him. He put his articles away and took his seat. As I sat back down we were joined by the third member of our row, an older woman who seemed to have the same disposition as he had when first arriving at the seat. She looked at me, sighed and sat down. The sigh was a little off putting in that it seemed directed at me and almost as if she was offended that she was sitting next to me.

The older gentleman leaned into me with a perturbed disposition, "When we planned this trip, our travel agent assured us that there was no one seated between us," the husband stated. At this point it was made clear that these two were traveling together and I felt somehow compelled to correct the situation. In the spirit of good travel, I thought I should offer to switch seats with one of them hoping that they would be much more comfortable seated next to each other than apart for the duration of the flight with a complete stranger seated between them.

"Would either of you like to switch so you can sit together?"

"No, we chose these seats specifically," he replied.

I thought the offer was courteous and somewhat generous considering the circumstances. We were about to spend several hours crossing the Atlantic Ocean and it made more sense to be closer to a loved one than divided by a stranger.

His wife never said a word to me nor acknowledged my presence other than to periodically inch her body away from mine at each and every opportunity to the point she was nearly in the aisle of the plane. The flight attendants had begun their final checks throughout the cabin as the captain prepared to take us into flight. I placed my headphones on and began my own preflight routine in order to psyche myself up for this journey and to tune out my new travel companions. I wasn't interested in conversation, but the impression that they had made with me was setting a tone in which I was certain that I did not want to know them any closer.

I found myself getting deeper into my thoughts and preparing for the time that I would have in London to complete more of my research and even catch some of the sites and visit several museums in the time that I would not busy conducting research. Despite my thoughts of what awaited me on the other side of the Atlantic, I was repeatedly distracted by this couple. I had grown accustomed, unfortunately, to when people did not want me around, but where was I supposed to go? Should I sit in the overhead bin so that they may have the middle seat all to themselves as they had assumed would be the case when they planned out their trip to Europe? Maybe if there was still time, I could ask the flight attendant to have me seated in the lavatory for the remainder of the flight, or perhaps the wing? Any and all of these options would work for this couple as it would make them much more comfortable about their seating situation. Frankly, they were making me uncomfortable with the way they were addressing and not addressing the predicament. I had offered them the opportunity to exchange seats which was met with a negative reply. It just seemed as though it was more of a bother to them than anything. What else was left but to enjoy sitting between those two crotchety people for the eight-hour flight? The plane took off and I was resigned to thinking about the limited amount of time that I would have over the next few days and how I would parcel it up between research and recreation.

As we reached the cruising altitude I removed my headphones and began scrawling more notes about relationship between Cuba, the United States and Great Britain during the 19th century. The flight attendants were moving around the cabin and selecting people to relocate to the business and first class section of the plane. In the back of my mind, I thought that this would be my chance to remove myself from a tense and uncomfortable situation, should a flight attendant be able to assist me. To my surprise, my row mate, was thinking the same thing, only with different motivations. He craned his neck over his shoulder watching people move from their seats as they were directed by the flight attendants to their upgraded status.

In a very disingenuous tone, he leaned in, pointing to several seats scattered in various rows behind us and said, "Hey pal, I think there are some seats opening up. I think you'd be more comfortable over there."

The declaration wasn't an issue of taking my comfort into consideration, it was more an assertion of his willingness to veil his discomfort with my presence by providing this gesture, this offering to somehow alleviate any and all tension within the situation. It wasn't about my comfort. It was about his comfort, more accurately, it was about his discomfort with me sitting next to him. Before I could fully even acknowledge or even respond to what he was stating, he was flagging the flight attendant over, raising up in his seat in order to ensure that he gained her full attention.

"Ma'am, is there another seat available for him?" *This asshole… Does he think that he is doing me a favor at this point?* "I just think he'd be much more comfortable in one of the open seats."

"Sure, we have some that have opened up."

Looking at me she stated, "Sir, if you would just follow me."

As the wife gave me space to pass by, I grabbed my things and followed the flight attendant to the rear of the aircraft. We walked roughly eight rows to my new location and I was introduced to where I was to be seated.

"Here you are."

"Excuse me…" *The entire row was empty. This can't be right.*

In a hushed tone, she further explained, "It's all

yours."

"Thank you," I replied with a bit of confusion.

As I sat down, she gave me a pat on the shoulder as if she understood the situation that had taken place between myself and the other passengers. It wasn't stated, but I felt as though it was understood. This more than likely was a situation that she had encountered more than once in her career and unfortunately, would likely not be the last time she had witnessed incidents such as this. The gentleman never explicitly stated that he didn't wanted to be seated next to me because of my skin color, but he never performed any action that would remove the doubt that this was a motivator. Maybe it is possible that I misread his behavior, but this was something that I was too familiar with. I had entered "his space" and I was unwelcome.

"Special" Kind of Guy

I have long been a lover of film. Much like the character Tom in Tennessee William's *Glass Menagerie,* I would often catch a movie in order to escape into the worlds that filmmakers create for us on-screen. One of my favorite jobs in college was working for a movie theater in that it allowed me to have access to films and discuss them with many of the patrons and my coworkers. As an historian, I fell in love with the various aspects of film and the role that they have in society.

Through a friend, I had the opportunity to attend film screenings in order to review them for his website and magazine. This afforded me the ability to express more about what I thought about the films and catch a few that I otherwise wouldn't get out to see if it weren't for the screenings. During one occasion, I had the opportunity to attend a screening for *Selma,* Ava Duvernay's dramatization of the 1965 Civil Rights March to gain voter protection for African-Americans. I had been looking forward to the release of this film since the day its production was announced. Despite being familiar with the story and history of the era, I was intrigued with how this would transfer onto film.

I entered and took my seat with the other media guests in our roped off section after chatting it up with the production team responsible for arranging the screening. I took out my notes and began my process of how I would evaluate the film. *Should I focus more on the history? Should I focus on the acting? Maybe I should look for some of the other historical and political criticisms that had already come out about the film with respect to Johnson's representation or even the changes that had to be made to the film because of licensing issues with Dr. King's speeches?* I continued to take notes and "game plan" my process before the rest of the guests arrived and the film started.

A few minutes after I had begun writing my notes, people started to trickle into the theater for general seating. As they entered, the production team informed them that there was open seating everywhere except the roped off section, which was reserved for media, special guests, etc. After attending several of these screenings, I had this procedure memorized. I was so used to it that I tuned out most of the background noise and continued to take my notes as the rest of the theater patrons found their seats.

With just a few minutes before the start of the movie, an older woman and her friend walked into the theater. She was openly frustrated and voiced it with the organizers of the screening. She complained as to why there were no seats left for her or her friend. She remarked that she was extremely embarrassed at the situation and that she had gone out of her way in order to ensure that her friend made it to this film. Each word that came out of her mouth was increasingly obnoxious and condescending. *Just keep your head down and ignore all that is happening. She just wants an audience in order to get some sort of sympathy from the theater or from the production company in order to receive compensation for her tardiness.*

I watched out of the corner of my eye as the events unfolded and immediately regretted sitting at the end of the row which put me five feet away from this situation. She scanned in my direction and continued to complain about the circumstances.

Please don't involve me in this. Please.

I began praying that I would not be singled out or brought into the storm that this woman was becoming. I had an uncanny feeling that somehow, despite my wishes and demeanor, that I would not be left alone. I could sense it.

"There is nowhere to sit? Why can't I sit over there?" she asked, pointing to the VIP/Special Guest Area in which I was seated in order to review the film along with several members of the audience.

"Ma'am, that is the seating for the special guests." This gentleman had answered this question to dozens of people over the past 30-45 minutes and was not given the chance to clarify that matter any further before he was cut off by this woman.

"Well… *he* doesn't look that special to me! Why does *he* get to sit here?"

I had returned to my notes so I wasn't looking directly at her and wasn't even sure if she was talking about me, but something made me feel as though she was directing her anger and frustration towards me. *Don't involve me in this bullshit, lady.* I made the mistake of looking up from my notes out of curiosity to meet her eyes and finger pointing directly at me.

"Excuse me. Can you tell me what makes *you* so special that *you* get to sit here?"

It was clear. She was not only talking about me, but now she was talking to me and involving me in this situation.

I suspected with her first comments that she was somehow involving me in this "personal affront" to her. *What the fuck just happened here? Did I magically get transported into kindergarten where this lady became my teacher and felt compelled to ask me why I was special? Was she actually confronting a grown man over a seat that he was entitled to have as part of his obligation in reviewing the film? Did I, without my knowledge, time travel into 1960s Alabama? The attendant had already explained to her that the area was reserved. That should be sufficient, but for some reason out of the roughly two dozen people in the same section in which I was seated, she chooses to hone in on me.*

I fought back the desire to call her every name in the book and thus stoop to her level of ignorance. Instead of referring to her as the self-centered, pretentious, pompous asshole as she was presenting herself to be and making more of a scene than she already had, I took the moment that she created and decided to add a little humor, albeit sarcastic and a bit snarky, to the conversation.

"Ma'am, what makes me special? Well… let's see. I'm a veteran and a History professor with type O positive blood. I think that makes me pretty special." Someone chuckled behind me as they overheard the confrontation.

"If you're referring to the reason as to why I am in this seat and in this section, I'm here to review the movie. If it is really that important for you to find a seat, the other person who was joining me to review this film isn't showing up so I don't think it would be a problem if you took the seats next to me that are vacant."

No eye contact was made… not a "thank you" for the offer… nothing. She didn't acknowledge anything I said. She took the opportunity to then enter the row, stepping over me in the process and then proceeded to ask the gentleman two seats down from me if she could sit next to him. He obliged her. She and her friend took the two seats before striking up a very cordial conversation as to what brought him to the theater and what he did for a living. Nothing confrontational. Nothing insulting. Her demeanor was completely different with this man who was there for the same exact reason as I was. He and I both had notebooks on our laps with notes scribbled on the pages. We were both dressed casually. The only striking difference between he and I was that he was an older white male. He was unthreatening. He was safe. He was a seat companion that was preferable to her.

I sat there in my seat as this woman who was a bit older than my mother made me think of the irony of this situation. She was here to watch a movie about tolerance, acceptance, and dignity yet here she was talking down to another human being and insulting him because he didn't seem "special" to her.

The opening credits began to roll and I continued to process the moment and how oblivious this woman was to what she had done. It may not have been done out of racial malice, but it would be hard for me to see it as a situation free from race. When she confronted the event manager, she was still cordial in her demeanor. There was nothing unpleasant about it other than, according to her perspective, the fact that she had nowhere to sit. Even as I offered the seats next to me, trying to laugh off her behavior, I thought about how quick she was to dismiss it and request the seats next to the other gentleman, who was white. I was good enough to accost but not good enough to sit next to. She needed a barrier between us even after building a wall.

I knew that in that moment, I was not being judged by the content of my character, nor given the chance or opportunity to be judged so. What disturbed me even more than the slight was that she made the effort to see this film about racial bias, bigotry, injustice, and social progress, yet didn't "see" me. My presence was an inconvenience to hers. I didn't belong there. I wasn't "special" enough.

Strange Fruit

I was fresh out of the military and beginning my transition back into civilian life. It had been a rough couple of months of job searches with little interest as to my candidacy. In late July, I received a phone call requesting an interview. When I arrived, I tried not to get my hopes up. I had my degrees, my experience and desire to teach and mentor.

With it being the middle of the Summer, I knew it would be rather difficult to land a job in education given that many of the vacancies would have been filled. The interview seemed so banal that upon walking out of the door, I began calculating and strategizing my next steps in searching for employment.

After what seemed like an instant, I was back in my car heading home thinking about every aspect that I could have improved upon in order to land the position. My cell phone rang. It was the principal on the other end. The job was mine. This was the first serious offer that had come to me. I would be teaching Social Studies for a Junior High in Mesa, Arizona. It was a great opportunity to return to the field of education after being in the military. It afforded me the opportunity to start over in a different region of the country. It was a corner of America that I had little knowledge of other than the old westerns my father watched.

The school was situated in a heavily Mormon district and racially, it was predominantly white (66%) with the highest racial minority being Hispanic (25%). The black student population hovered just above 5%. When I first traveled out to Arizona, my girlfriend at the time made it a point to let me know how few black people there were in Arizona. I didn't fully believe her until I started to feel as though I was in my own personal game of "Where's Waldo?" Each time I came across another black person there was the mutual head nod; an acknowledgment that we knew what the other was thinking.

I had just moved from the south where it was not too uncommon to have areas where the black populations ranged anywhere from 30 - 60%, sometimes even higher, depending on the area. Having spent the majority of my life in the south, these demographics were so foreign to me. I looked forward, although anxiously, to the culture shock. I was curious as to what this change in diversity and circumstances would bring. This curiosity and excitement would quickly turn to disappointment.

During the first couple of months, there had been little turbulence other than what teachers typically deal with. As we closed in on the days leading up to the election, some students made grumblings about the choice which featured Senators John McCain and Barack Obama. With it being Arizona, many of the students were pulling for the local candidate, many others voiced their preference for Senator Obama. When asked of my opinion of the matters, I often deflected the issue and moved on. I never thought it was my place to discuss my personal political stances in a professional setting, much less with my students.

When teaching History, it's important to teach the good, as well as, the bad. We can't afford to avoid topics and themes because they make us uncomfortable. It is important to teach the parts that not everyone is willing to stomach and come to grips with the past. We should teach and learn from the It is vital to ensure that you expose your students to issues and concepts that ensures that they get the full picture of what history is and why it is important. This is how we become honest with history and ourselves.

When we reached the Fall of that year, we began our post-Civil War/Reconstruction and Jim Crow Era section where my students learned about segregation, discrimination, and even acts of racial violence. Days before I planned out the lesson and the photos that I would use to explain the concepts we would cover. The one that most concerned me was with respect to lynching. I was concerned, not about exposing them to the idea of violence, because the whole course was about violence. Each section that we seemed to cover discussed violence at some length. The films and documentaries for the course had scenes of violence that demonstrated to the students what was taking place during the time period and why it was taking place. It displayed the reality for many people during these periods.

I began the lesson discussing why lynching occurred and the response by groups such as the NAACP and the Urban League. We discussed the contributions of individuals like Ida B. Wells who fought hard against lynching and what they represented. My students read over the lyrics to "Strange Fruit" by Billie Holliday with the song playing in the background so that they might gain a greater grasp of how deep this issue was at the time. They understood and discussed why someone felt justified in doing this to another human being. Some of them in their "Roundtable" discussions questioned why someone would feel threatened by another person wanting to vote or even have the right to vote. They questioned what was so scary about this. There was real mature discussion happening with these kids. For them it became clear that lynching was not just an act of violence. It was an act of hate. It was brutal. It was an aspect of history that we should never repeat.

As the discussion continued, I tried to bring the

issue full circle and talk about how there was the attempt to stop people from voting through poll taxes, literacy tests, violence, or intimidation and then compared it with the reality that there was now an African-American Presidential Candidate for a major party. In this discussion, I brought up how there were many people who grew up during segregation and were intimidated or victims of violence when they wanted to exercise their right to vote. There were many people who, although witnessing or experiencing this violence, would now bear witness to and experience something that they could have never imagined. Most of the students understood how this was a change in history that was so remarkable for people who had been marginalized and left behind. One student did not see it the same way nor did it seem as though she wanted to.

"We have a nation where people, because of their racial background and gender, have gone from being prevented from voting through all types of methods, including lynching, to the possibility of electing an African-American Presidential candidate on one ticket and a female Vice-Presidential candidate on the other ticket."

"That's what they should do to Obama," one of my female students blurted out.

"What do you mean? Do what?"

"Lynch him. I think we should lynch Obama." There was no doubt or uncertainty in her voice. She made the statement as calmly as if she were ordering her lunch.

I was dumbfounded not knowing where this was coming from. We had just covered lynching, what it meant, how it affected communities, how destructive it was, and here she was proposing it for Senator Obama.

"You do understand what lynching is, right?"

"Yeah, and I don't care. That's what we should do to him"

Hearing these words come out of anyone's mouth was disappointing, to hear it in 2008 was disheartening, but to hear them come out of a 7th grade girl's mouth redefined the meaning of disgust. The room was silent and all eyes were looking at this one kid in her moment of what could only be deemed as ignorance at the time. Before we could have some resolution, the bell rang and all students dispersed.

After my students left the room, I was unsure of myself and what course of action to take, if any. I had a free period and went to speak with my Department Chair. Luckily, she was showing her students a film and could step out of her room to speak with me for a moment. I explained the situation to her and I stated that I was thinking of talking with her parents, but didn't know how to approach it. This was the first case in which I had a student make a disgusting comment like that in my room endorsing any type of violence toward anyone. She was just as dumbfounded as I was and could not wrap her head around this situation.

Still unclear of what course of action to pursue, I headed back to my room and punched out a quick email informing the Principal of the incident and my possible plan of action. Her response surprised me. Despite the description of what happened, she was hesitant to go forward with even contacting the parents. I simply informed her that my concern was not that she made a threat to anyone, but she made a statement like this openly and that if this were my child, I would want to be informed of it so it could be corrected. I was shocked and disappointed that this administrator was so dismissive of the concern. Despite this, I continued on by contacting the student's parents.

The call was difficult and I explained to her mother what had happened and why I was concerned. What happened next in her response took me completely by surprise;

"Lynching? She knows better than that! Why would she say something like? We don't teach her to act out violently. We don't support Obama or agree with him, but I would never approve of her saying something like this."

"I understand, ma'am. I was just concerned because she has never said anything like this before in class or acted out in this way. I just thought that you should know and I would want to know if I were in your place."

"This really bothers me. Some of her best friends are black. You're her favorite teacher. I don't understand why she would say something like this."

At that moment, I started to hear all of the same excuses about racial transgressions, whether large or small. *If you have black friends or someone in authority whom you like is black, then you cannot possibly be racist or have racist feelings, right?* This often causes people to be blind to the existence of social realities. It's just as pointless to bring up your friend of color in order to dispute any racial infractions as saying that you do not "see race."

She continued, "The only thing I can think of is that they have been discussing the anti-Christ at church. Maybe that is why she said this. I'm going to have to talk with someone at the Church and ask them about this."

The anti-Christ?

I tried not to laugh or even entertain the

attempted link. I found it odd that she would even make this connection to my lecture and a Church sermon. After I thought about it for a moment, I recalled that from the moment Senator Obama had announced his candidacy, he had received all sorts of personal attacks. I had heard on a couple of occasion where churches were teaching that he himself was the Antichrist and that parishioners should be prepared for the end times. All of this just sounded ridiculous to me until I found the email. *The anti-Christ was coming and he would be a man, in his 40s, of MUSLIM descent. He would deceive the nations with persuasive language, and have a MASSIVE Christ-like appeal....the prophecy says that people will flock to him and he will promise false hope and world peace, and when he is in power, he will destroy everything! Is it OBAMA??*

I laughed at the absurdity of it all. I found it all funny until I sat back, reflecting on the fact that there were people gullible and hate-filled enough to believe the words in the message.

We continued the conversation where she resolved to talk to her daughter about it and follow up later. A few days had passed since the incident when I received a message on my school voicemail which was cause for concern. The girl's mother had called. The tone in her voice was very confused, short and worried. In turn it made me anxious. She wanted me to call her as soon as possible.

After I dialed the number, she answered without letting a full ring pass. There were no pleasantries or introductions made.

"Mr. G., you didn't, by chance, tell anyone what my daughter said, did you?"

"Specifically, your daughter, no. I spoke with another teacher and an administrator to inform them about the situation and seek guidance, but I never mentioned her name, nor her gender. I simply identified her as 'a student' when speaking of the situation," I explained.

"Well, I don't know what to think. Someone came up to me the other day when I was picking up my daughter. He patted me on the back stating he heard about what she said in class. Another man came up to me and praised me for what happened saying, 'You're raising your daughter right. That's exactly what we should do to Obama.' It shocked me because I have never met this man and he knew about what happened in your classroom."

"I assure you that I never mentioned your daughter's name to anyone, nor have I mentioned this to anyone other than those I was seeking guidance from. With that being said, your daughter said this in a room full of other students many of whom are her friends which is why I called you when it happened initially.

These kids talk and things like this spread quickly."

The mother was concerned about her reputation as a parent and the people that her child was surrounded by. The situation opened her eyes to this new reality. For myself, it made me even more uneasy about the whole situation. Instead of quelling the situation, as I had hoped, it had now exposed the ignorance and prejudice that existed within the household of at least one other child in my class.

PLAY BALL!!!

Full disclosure: I am a horrible athlete and have little to no coordination. My best athletic feats have taken place on PlayStation. With that being said, I cannot sit down and enjoy a professional or collegiate game without someone approaching me to inquire about my athletic career.

This is not to be confused with the mundane conversations that people typically have with strangers seated near them during a game who discover that they make up the same fan base. Inquiries about my athletics begin upon my entry into the arenas and stadiums for football, baseball, and basketball.

"You look familiar."

"I get that a lot."

"Oh, I know. You used to play ball here!"

"No. I actually work here."

"Oh. So, you coach? Which sport?"

Or…

"What sport did you play here?"

"None."

"I know. You used to wrestle here."

"No. I teach history here."

"Are you sure? You're pretty big. I bet you used wrestle here."

Uncomfortable Silence

There are some moments that come across your life that make you wonder their purpose. You question why you needed to be a part of them. What is it that caused you to have to bear witness to this? Sometimes it is for the humor, others it is for the mere learning experience.

One moment that stays etched in my memory occurred during a session of my AP Chemistry class in high school. As would be the case with many of my experiences over my high school, college, and professional career, I was the only minority in the room.

Having an instructor who seemed to be more concerned with impressing her students most of the time, various topics came up for debate during class that had little to do with what we were learning throughout the course. Some of the topics pushed some of my more religious classmates into furious debate over them. Sometimes I engaged. Sometimes I sat back and watched the fireworks. One such discussion morphed into the topic of abortion. Britt, one of the students who was the daughter of a Southern Baptist preacher and always confrontational about matters that conflicted with her beliefs took to this topic rabidly. Several other students jumped in and confronted her as she began to reference the Bible and religion as reason enough for her to oppose such a practice. Moments like this made me question why she was even taking this science course given her religious convictions.

Our teacher, taking the opportunity to engage her further as to why she thought this way began to ask her for any possible scenarios in which either she or her family would support abortion. She wanted to know if there was any way in which she would change her mind on the issue. Each question, scenario, prompt and idea was met with a "no" reply. I just sat there as I knew that this conversation was going to continue or even morph into something else so I didn't even bother trying to complete the lab assignment. I figured that if it didn't matter to the teacher, it shouldn't matter to me.

As she continued confronting this topic with her student, my instructor looked over in my direction and then looked back at Britt and asked a question I, to this day, felt should have not been posed. She took the time to formulate the strategy. There was nothing abrupt about the moment when she asked it. She thought this out.

"Well, let's say you were, well…" She turned to look at me, paused and continued, "raped by a black man. Would you or your parents change their view on abortion then?"

She didn't make it about a sick child.

She didn't make it about a dying mother.

She didn't make it about how there was a choice that was affecting one or the other.

She didn't even make it just about rape.

She made it about more than rape.

She made it about rape by a black man.

In that moment, she made the crime and the race linked. She further cemented long held fears and beliefs that there is some intrinsic threat from black males that they will uncontrollably rape you when given the chance. She had transcended the issue of race and created this racial association with the crime and behavior. Even worse, she ensured that there was somehow something worse about rape if it had been committed by a black assailant on a white female. For this young girl, it should allow her to break from her religious convictions due to the possibility that she might be impregnated by a black male due to rape.

At my lab space, I sat there and watched as she tried to process the scenario and as my teacher sat back and awaited a response. As I sat there, I saw that everyone else in that room had missed the association that had been presented and the misrepresentation and mischaracterization of a people. It was treated so matter-of-factly. I sat there and under my breath remarked "Not just a rapist, but a black rapist," hoping someone else understood the problem in the situation as it was presented. Nothing… Not a word from my peers… No eye contact or acknowledgement of what had been said.

Britt was still trying to process the question posed to her. Each previous prompt had been so simple. Her responses had all followed the same line of, "No, I don't believe in that." Or "No. That is against my faith." This had her stalled. With her fumbling over her response, I decided to take the initiative. It was clear that no one noticed the problematic affront that our instructor had laid out and I felt it was somehow my responsibility to bring the attention to the issue. As everyone was waiting for her to contemplate, I cut through the tension that was building and present in that room.

"Would it make it easier if I left and went out into the hall?"

I was met with blank stares. There was no understanding of the words that had just come out of my mouth by my classmates or by my teacher so I elaborated.

"Well, if you're concerned with black people being rapists and not rapists in general, then you might not want the only black student present when it's decided that the race is the reason that someone decides to be a hypocrite."

With that, I walked out of the room and waited for the bell to ring so I could proceed to my next class. Nothing was said to me about the incident. No one discussed my comments with me any further. I didn't even know if I made my point at that moment. All I know is that at that moment, in that room, I felt as though I was singled out as though I was somehow a potential criminal lurking in the shadows who was only driven by sexual desires. "I fit the description."

In an instant, I felt that this was how my teacher saw me. I felt that was how some of my female classmates saw me or people like me. I didn't feel as though I was seen as an equal or someone who deserved to be in that room due to my academic ability. I was made to feel lesser than my peers. This same teacher was shocked when it was brought to her attention that many of my white peers would get drunk, high, and be involved in any number of nefarious activities in and out of school. They were the "good kids." She dismissed any of the stories that my classmates told her as false. They all came from good, stable families, so there was no possibility in her mind that any of them could be throwing parties in which alcohol and drugs were in regular use. Despite this, she continued the narrative that the black kids, especially the young black males, were the dangerous ones. We were the only ones who were consumed with violence and capable of such degenerate activities as rape. We were the bad ones, the ones whose sole occupation would be lurking in the dark waiting to prey on some poor innocent soul. This moment continued a legacy of perpetuating a long held negative attribute onto black males and black identity.

Don't Overdo It

My phone rang. When I answered it, I was met with Celine exclaiming her outrage on the other end.

"Oh, people are so stupid!"

No "hello" or "How are you doing?"

"I can't believe this!!!"

"What?"

"My family and I were sitting down to eat at a restaurant when my niece tapped me on the arm. 'C.C., that man over there keeps saying really bad words.' I asked her what she heard and she says that he was saying the N-Word! I looked over in his direction and heard the man continuing his conversation. 'N this' and 'N that!' It was disgusting!"

And what am I supposed to do about this?

"Well, I got up from the table and confronted him. I told him that his behavior was unacceptable and that my boyfriend is black. He should not be speaking like this. It's 2005 and this is unacceptable!"

"Wow."

"I know!"

"When did this happen?"

"About five minutes ago."

"Wait… Where are you?"

"Still in the restaurant waiting for our food to come."

If you are our friend or ally, there really is no need to tell us of every instance in which you defend black people when we are not around. There is little need to inform us of the situation. If you correct an indiscretion or confront someone over their bigotry, you don't need to report back to any of us. We are not keeping score to see who is "down with the cause."

Hair... Don't touch it... Don't think about touching it...

Jared sat one row over from me in Algebra class. I never talked to the guy, nor had we ever had any interaction despite being in several of the same classes Freshman year. He turned to me with no prompting, looking me over.

"Hey. How do you wash your hair?"

The fuck kind of question is that?

"What do you mean?"

"How do you wash your hair?"

I didn't have a special haircut nor any crazy designs. It was a simple crop, nothing fancy. I didn't understand what would prompt him to ask the question. In responding to him, I could only think of one reasonable answer. I leaned into him so there was no confusion.

"Lather. Rinse. Repeat."

He then moved his hand closer to me and was within an inch of my scalp. I flinched.

"What are you doing?"

"I wanted to touch it. It looks so soft almost like wool." He stretched a bit more almost tilting his seat sideways.

"Don't touch my hair."

"Why? I just wanted to see how it felt."

"I am not a plaything or an animal for your inspection."

This guy really put himself out there in the middle of our class. He went from curiosity to a full-on invasion of personal space. Hair is, especially in the black community, a "touchy" subject. Questions are fine. Interest is fine. Petting is a no-no.

We can't even touch a black woman's hair during the most intimate of moments. What makes you think that you can pet someone during a casual interaction?

"Soul Shake"

When going in for the handshake, just go in for a handshake. Don't attempt anything you saw in a rap video, on YouTube, something you saw the kids at the mall doing or anything that you think would be cool to try... just shake my hand...

If I don't know you, or more specifically, I don't "know" you, the handshake is not going to be awarded upon the first encounter. If I had a dollar for every time someone tried to give me their version of the "soul shake" upon first meeting me, I would have been retired before entering college.

SPF 100

I don't care about your tan. I really don't. I never will. I will care even less about you when you walk up to me, pointing at your skin, and utter the words "Look, I'm almost as dark as you!"

Skin color is a sensitive issue in general. There are so many issues relevant to identity wrapped up into these layers of dermis and shades of melanin. Coming to me and then bragging about how you are now almost as "dark as me" does not present itself as a sign of kinship. It is seen as mocking, disrespectful and a little obnoxious. In fact, as soon as the words come out of your mouth, I am willing a sunburn your way and hoping for every store to have run out of Aloe Vera.

While we're on the subject of skin… No matter what shade we are, black people get "ashy." Due to this, we do not keep lotion in stock within our homes. We all have healthy supplies of Shea and Cocoa Butter in our pantries, bathrooms, bedrooms, cars, desk drawers, and various assorted compartments. We prefer "the butters" and, if you are "old school," Vaseline. Cocoa butter and Shea butter do wonders to ensure that our skin is fully moisturized and prevents us from any embarrassing moments with our friends in which our "ashy" skin will be pointed out. No one wants to have their knees and elbows look like they have been crawling through chalk.

Supporting Cast

Yes, some of us talk at the movies. We're not going to stop anytime soon. I made the mistake of trying to "Shush" my mother on one occasion. I still have the scars, both physical and emotional, from the incident. The reality is that movies are entertainment and an interactive experience. In many cases, it is an extension of the community and shared experience, much like church.

My friend James had the pleasure of experiencing this first hand. He and I checked out a horror film in the Black and Hispanic part of Phoenix once. His reaction to the "show" was priceless. He was more entertained by the commentary coming from the audience than the plot and action from the film.

As we exited the auditorium, he looked at me asking, "Is it always like that?"

"Like what?"

"That entertaining?"

"Pretty much. Black audiences have added entertainment value."

"I haven't laughed that hard in a long time. My sides still hurt. From now on we have to watch movies here.

This is the greatest audience I have ever been around."

A word to the wise; join in on this adventure or sit back and enjoy the commentary and reactions of those seated near you. Then again, you could just wait and watch the film in the privacy of your own home. In that case, I guarantee you that it won't be as enjoyable as watching it with a packed auditorium of people conversing back with the actors onscreen and reacting to each and every moment of the film.

We talk in church and that's free admission. What makes you think any of us are going to keep quiet during a horror, action, or comedy flick when we are paying ten dollars for a ticket?

"SPEAK SO WELL"

The local news came by to pay our theater a visit. As we were heading into the Summer movie season, they wanted to hold interviews about the coming attractions for a feature they planned to air. As their reporter began speaking to the manager, he pointed to me.

"That's your guy right there."

Jerry was reluctant to perform the interview. He didn't want to go on camera. Within seconds of him pointing in my direction, a camera and microphone were in my face. I didn't like being put on the spot and I liked being volunteered even less. Anxiety started to consume my mind. I thought about how this video would be on air for the local community which, from my dealings, had not ascended beyond a 1950s mindset.

The reporter began his line of questioning and I informed him of all the films that our audiences could expect in the coming months. There was a healthy amount of action, comedic, and family films the local community would have the opportunity to enjoy.

When the segment wrapped, I was relieved that it had concluded. I gave little thought to my contribution other than what time it would air and have the ability to catch it on television. I didn't think anything that I said was profound, though-provoking, or interesting in the slightest.

The weekend passed and I had missed my opportunity to catch the feature on television. With my work schedule that weekend I had hoped to at least catch the local broadcast at least once or even hear from one of my coworkers who had caught the segment. Unfortunately, no one I knew had the opportunity of seeing it. I had started to think that it hadn't aired. If someone saw it, they surely would have busted my chops a little for being a "celebrity."

A few more days had passed and my thoughts about the interview were far from my mind. I would be quickly reminded of the interview and have a new sense of disgust as a result.

It was slow for a Sunday, which was strange as we had a good number of newly released films. As I made my rounds, cleaning and organizing areas of the theater, I noticed the girlfriend of one of my co-workers had walked in. She was carrying his lunch as she seemed to always do. Instead of walking toward the office, as was her routine, she was walking in my direction. I found it odd. We never had a conversation. I didn't recall ever saying anything more than hello to her from the time that I had worked there. We never had any significant interactions. Her boyfriend and I didn't associate with each other. We were simply coworkers.

He didn't get in my way. I didn't get in his. I found it peculiar that she would have something to say to me in the first place.

> "Hey, me and my family saw you on TV the other day."
>
> "Really? I missed it."
>
> "My dad was so impressed. He wanted to know where you learned to speak so well."

Impressed? Were they thinking that this was some parlor trick that I pulled off? I had somehow rehearsed this over and over in order to appear as some sort of oddity which hopes to amaze his crowds? I was just answering questions as any subject of an interview does.

I had heard these responses all too often and was never prepared to deal with it nor accustomed to this type of commentary. I had been described this way for years and it never sat well with me. When she said this to me and asked the question inquiring as to where I happened to learn how to speak "this way." I was annoyed, frustrated and insulted. I was a cultural anomaly. I was an outlier. I wanted to be polite in response to this ignorance. Part of me wanted to be petty and condescending. That side won.

With a smile on my face and a touch of sarcasm and contempt in my voice, I responded. "Well, funny you should ask. I went to school and got an education."

Her bright, chipper demeanor shielded her from the comment and continued her ability to remain unaware of the meaning behind her words or those of her parents.

"Ok," she said as she turned and bounced her way to the office. The tone of her "ok" was closer to "Cool! I'll tell my folks as soon as I see them," completely oblivious to her actions or the tone behind my words.

What bothered me more than her words was that her father, as I had learned from all of our mutual friends, was the principal of the local high school. We were in southeast Georgia where the opportunities were limited and the expectations were even more restricted. It was a community with a history of racial inequality and discrimination. Despite having so much contact between the white and black communities, there was little contact that went beyond the surface. Tropes, generalizations, and stereotypes are allowed to flourish in order to demean and dehumanize groups. It attributes ignorance to black voices and skin.

"You're so articulate. You speak so well." On the surface, it sounds like something that is so mundane and inconsequential, but there is more to it. It minimizes the other person's identity and intellect. The comment does not elevate them, rather it indicates that you are surprised that they were able to speak with any sense of annunciation and elocution. You want the people to conform to the stereotypes that you are accustomed to and are taken aback when someone exceeds them. What you are telling me or anyone else who receives this "compliment" is "I totally thought you were going to mangle the English language. Wow! I am so happy that you speak like this and not like some ghetto trash."

It is treated as though we are speaking another language and the other party is surprised and astonished that we can communicate. *Hooray! We are able to speak the same language! I can understand you!* The praise is a virtual pat on the head. The only thing missing is the exclamation of "Good Boy" and handing us a treat. Somehow, this ability to communicate now gives us a sense of kinship and now the guard that they would typically put up comes down because we are the "safe ones."

If you ever find yourself immediately feeling compelled to state "he's so articulate" or "she speaks so well," don't do it. Stop yourself before the words come out of your mouth. Cut them off at the vocal cords and synapses that control this motor function.

Calling someone, especially a person of color, "articulate" or stating that "they speak so well" is not a compliment at all. It is something that will cause us to recoil and become somewhat defensive and feel as though you are about to pat us on the head. In fact, that is what this is. It is a virtual pat on the head for not being a stereotype in your eyes. If we are great speakers, talk about the speech that we gave or the content of what we delivered. We don't need to hear about how we were able to annunciate properly. Exceptions can be made if we are being evaluated as part of a Speech and Debate course or competition, but it shouldn't be your initial reaction to hearing someone speak.

"Incognegro"

It was set. Evander Holyfield and Lennox Lewis were having their rematch for the heavyweight title and this bout was hailed to be even bigger than the last one. The fight would result in the first undisputed Heavyweight Champion in over 6 years. The fight was even titled "Unfinished Business" to drive the message home that these two were out to finish each other off. None of us wanted to miss this fight and Jeff decided that he would order it and turn it into an excuse for us all to get together and drink, cook out and have a good time.

I arrived at his house that night ready to watch Lewis beat Holyfield and take the title. This was a cardinal sin with the company I was keeping considering Holyfield was the American fighter and from Atlanta, which was just a three-hour drive away from campus. There was a good crowd that showed up for the fight. People had their plates of food, beer, some were smoking outside, but all were having a good time. As I looked around, that thought entered my head, "I'm the only splash of color here. Oh well." It was something that I had become accustomed to.

The prefight speculation had started and everyone had begun taking their seats, and moving into their nooks in order to get ready for the fight. I was a little late to picking my spot on any of the couches so I sat against the wall which, as it turned out, was quite comfortable. I had another sip of my beer and bite of a burger and awaited the entrances of Holyfield and Lewis.

Jim Lampley, George Foreman, and Larry Merchant were discussing the two fighters and what to expect from them. They ran down their stats and the men were announced for their entrances. Lewis walked down to the ring with no robe and was stone-faced giving you no indication that he was intimidated by the stage or circumstances. Evander Holyfield then began his trek to the ring wearing a purple poncho. As they stood in the ring and awaited the completion of the full introductions, I couldn't predict or expect what would happen in that room. "The Real Deal, Holyfield!!!!" the announcer broadcast to the crowd. At the same time, Holyfield took off his poncho revealing his physique.

"GODDAMN!!! THAT NIGGER'S IN SHAPE!"

"HOLY SHIT! THAT IS ONE HUGE NIGGER!"

What the Fuck?!?!?! I couldn't have possibly heard that. They couldn't have possibly said that…I have to be imagining this. Maybe I am just hypersensitive due to being the only person of color in the room. This is 1999! We are about to enter a new Millennium! We are getting closer to

Star Trek, yet not gaining distance from bigotry and ignorance.

At that moment, I questioned the validity of what I had heard and even what I should do about it. Everything in that moment for me stopped. I couldn't even taste the food that I had just bitten into. In so many situations one would expect that this would cause those who were in the room to stop what they were doing and possibly correct the "infraction" made by the others in the room, but this was not the case. I was alone in my disgust and disappointment. I looked around the room. Everyone continued watching the fight. There was no dispute that these statements had been said. There was little confusion that it had been heard by anyone else. No one said anything about it. No one wanted to acknowledge what these guys were doing despite the volume in which they expressed themselves.

They were guests just as I was and this to me reflected the acceptable attitude and perceptions of my hosts. My eyes veered from the television again to look around and it was then that I realized, everyone forgot I was here. I am here in the back of the room near the corner out of most people's line of sight. I had become "Incognegro." I couldn't blow my cover in order to see how far this would go. If someone was willing to be this free with their use of "nigger," I wondered what else they would say as long as they didn't know I was in the room. I had "snuck" backstage to my own existence. I was receiving an exclusive access to "behind the scenes."

What was going to happen? What would I experience? Who else was going to show their "true colors" and start hurling epithets tonight? Was anyone going to step forward? If not, am I going to be stuck with the burden of pointing out this transgression and propose some sort of rectification or prompt some action by my white "friends" in attendance? When were they going to notice that I was here? How long was it going to take?

I continued watching the fight just as everyone else, but I remained aware of my surroundings. My eyes and ears were wide open with respect to any offenses should they arise. Racial Slurs and epithets kept coming from several of the people in the room. These were the people I worked with. These were people I had gone to school with. These were people I had once considered friends. I found myself even more disappointed in the company I was keeping. My suspicions and fears had been confirmed.

The rounds wore on as Holyfield and Lewis battered each other with jabs and uppercuts. They were living up to the hype. And then it happened. In one of the later rounds Lennox Lewis landed an uppercut on Holyfield that stunned him.

"DAM! HE ALMOST KNOCKED THAT NIGGER OUT! HE WAS FUCKING HIM UP THAT ROUND."

I looked up and to my right, Sean was pouring himself a drink. At this moment, something must have clicked for him. He looked up in my direction only to find me looking over in his. There was nothing for him to say or do at this moment. He and Jeff were hosting this night and he just realized what had been occurring. As he looked at me, his eyes said enough. It was a look that was halfway between "Oh shit" and "I'm so sorry." He never once had uttered a slur, but he knew that even though he hadn't been in the wrong for what had been said, he could have spoken up. He failed to do so. In not speaking up, he condoned the words. He became complicit in his guests' actions. He rendered himself as a coconspirator in white supremacy.

Moments like this cause us to question our friends and their true thoughts about us. Although neither of the friends that I was close with had been the ones to make the comments or statements, they did condone it by not addressing those who said it. We often work in the logic of "guilt by association." With that being said, it is understood that by not coming forward against and saying something to their friends who attended the party, it makes one assume that they have those same feelings and perspective.

This changed the perception I had of all my friends who had attended that party from that moment on. Although there had been several who had not made racial remarks or participated in any of the bigotry, the bond was broken. Having my "fly on the wall" moment allowed me to see how my friends operated when I was not around. That glimpse revealed what I feared was the reality. They did not reject bigotry and ignorance, rather, they tolerated it under their own roofs and did not address it when given the opportunity. It was treated no differently than breathing. Being an ally against ignorance is not conditional.

No Joking Matter

Just because we are friends does not mean that you can unleash any and all racial jokes, commentary, or rants to or around me. Once that seal of racial security is broken, our interaction will be forever spoiled. I am not sure what would compel one to think that telling me a "black joke" or a "Mexican joke" or an "Asian joke" or any other racially/culturally offensive joke in a professional or social setting would be ok, especially if it isn't even funny.

Having that friend of a specific background does not give you access or ability to offend, nor is it going to make you immune to whatever reaction may come about. Unless you are a comedian and I am paying to hear these jokes, keep them to yourself, otherwise, I am always going to be suspicious of your motivations in telling me why there is cotton in a bottle of aspirin.

"What should I call you?"

Identity is a peculiar thing. Most people don't give it much thought unless speaking specifically about their particular heritage or family history. For many African-Americans, this is an issue that we have struggled with for generations. We've been referred to as Negroes, Colored, Black, Afro-American, and African-American. The change in the nomenclature may be confusing and sometimes unsettling for people outside of the black community and to an extent, those within the community. There are names, titles, terms, nicknames associated that break down the varying shades of skin color within the race. Additionally, there are the various ethnicities and cultural backgrounds that encompass the identity and define what it means to be "black."

There have been several times in which my identity, heritage, race, and background have been questioned. Each time seems to be more interesting than the last. In one instance I was in the home of my then girlfriend's grandparents. Delbert and Ruby Mays had settled in Arizona during the late 1950s. During their time in Arizona, and considering the demographics and societal constraints, they had very little meaningful interaction with any black people. It was quite noticeable in the way that they would cater their language in our conversations. According to their family, I had been the first black person in their home (This was far from a "Jackie Robinson Moment," but worth noting).

During one conversation, Del began telling me about some work that he had done around the house years before and how he had a friend who had helped him with it. Anyone who has had the pleasure of sitting down with their grandparents knows that the stories they tell are never going to be done within a certain allotted time.

"He's a nice fellah. He's a bla… African-American too."

I just smirked as he continued on with his story.

"Well, he was helping me fix the..." he trailed off again to the point where I lost track of the substance of our conversation.

I continued to listen to the story and it happened again. Just as before, I gave him a smirk and lightly chuckled at the awkwardness in the way that the conversation was going. However, this was no different than most of our conversations and interactions. He would often laugh about something and then just carry on with his story. Something about our conversation struck his wife and she felt the need to chime in.

"What's so funny you two?"

"Nothing, just you don't have to keep pausing when describing your friend or me, and you don't have to bring up my race when doing so."

"What do you mean?"

"Well, whenever you guys talk about me, you say 'he's a black…African-American.' You pause as if you are correcting yourself from trying to not be offensive."

"But you are, aren't you?"

"Am I what?

"African-American. You *are* African-American, ain't ya?"

"Yes…But, I don't start off conversations that way or introduce myself as such. I don't walk up to people and say. 'Hi there, I'm an African-American, nice to meet you.' It doesn't make any sense."

"Can we not say black?"

In the back of my mind I thought as to why they would need my permission to say anything, not to mention, they had used black as an identifier so many times before.

"You can say black if you want, but that's not the issue."

"Well, do you want to be called black or African-American? What should I call you?"

"My name. You can call me by my name."

It took a minute to sink in for them. My race was not something that they were to use as this dispensable tool in order to identify me or anyone else. It definitely is something to bring up as part of someone's identity and history, but it is not the complete makeup of an individual. There is much more to the person than that one identifier. This would be like describing a book and only saying what genre it belonged to.

It is commendable that someone is sensitive to the changing times and trying to understand the new standards when it comes to the way in which people are identified or wish to be identified. This is not something that is as simple as nationality or even ethnicity in which there is much more rigidity.

The titles are something that can have more room for fluidity and offer the opportunity for growth and represent the full awareness and reclamation of an identity that so many African-American were denied for generations. It is something that may continue to evolve and change over time, but is much deeper than just the term being applied.

Name Game

My history teacher started reading from the roll as a way to identify who he was going to be dealing with for the year. It seemed so mundane and uneventful. It was something that was taking place in classrooms around the country during the first day of school. I looked around the room and again, found myself as one of a handful of students of color. It is something I was seemingly always subject to and cognizant of.

"When I call your name, say 'here.' If there is another name that you go by, please let me know."

He proceeded to roll through the names and then came to mine.

"Donald Guillory?"

"Present… but it's D.J."

"Dequan?"

"No. D.J."

"DeJohn?"

"No. Deee Jaaaay."

"DeJayn?"

I thought that he must have been pulling my leg at this point. I didn't mumble, stutter, or stammer when saying my nickname. It was something I had had for well over ten years at this point and had to advise my teachers of since I was first put into a class with another Donald.

"No. D period. J period."

"D.J.? But there is no 'J' in your name."

"Yes. Donald Junior. I'm named after my father, Donald Senior."

"Oh. That's it? I thought your name was more exotic. I thought you were a 'Dijon' or something. Alright, D.J. it is."

From his countenance, he seemed disappointed that I wasn't a condiment. It didn't dawn on him that I had a "normal" name. I had a good number of friends whose names were unique. Unfortunately, when your name is "different," people find a way to ridicule this individuality and personal expression.

Despite the name that was on the roster, he was willing me to have, in his words, "something more exotic" like some of my peers. I was supposed to have a name that he could ridicule or mock. No matter how banal or unique someone's name may be, it is still their name. Learn it. Learn how to pronounce it. It is literally who they are. No matter how hard you may think someone's name is to pronounce or spell, make the effort.

Wakeup Call

Growing up I only heard about the trouble that other black males had with the police and the justice system from a distance. I had never been in serious trouble in school nor had I ever had any interactions or scrapes that would have ever involved the police. I was considerably naïve to what it was like firsthand. My knowledge came from my parents, family, and their friends when discussing what dealing with the police was like.

While in High School, my mother reinforced the belief that I needed to work hard in school to get ahead. Being diligent and staying clear of trouble, she was certain, would ensure a smooth path to success for me. She was born in Virginia to sharecropper parents and joined the ARMY once she graduated High School. She and other relatives would often tell me about the hardship of growing up in a state and a nation where they were often judged and mistreated because of the color of their skin. At the time, I thought we had grown past this. I was attending a moderately affluent and relatively diverse High School. I was making good grades and enrolled in honors courses throughout my time there. I made it a point to stay out of trouble.

Despite my wishes, trouble came looking for me

one night.

During my Junior year, I had a part-time job which often required me to work late. The job was typical for the time and something that most teenagers would complain about, but it gave me the chance to earn some money and get out of the house a few nights a week. One of my friends and I worked together there and often matched up our working schedules. One of the days that we were working was a little slower than others and especially odd for a weekend so I was asked to clock out early. Because my friend and I rode to work together, as we sometimes did, I waited until his schedule ended in order to leave.

The route to Jay's house from work was different than the one I would take directly home as he lived much closer than I did. As we were driving, I noticed that we were coming up on a neighborhood where I had first lived when I arrived in Georgia a few years earlier. I informed my friend of the discovery and turned down the subdivision's entrance. After a couple of turns, I passed by my old house. It was then that I noticed a couple of cars further down the street. I felt a bit uneasy and I turned the truck around and headed back out of the neighborhood. Something didn't feel right. I questioned why the cars were blocking the street in this manner. I thought it was strange and that whoever it was, they probably had bad intentions. All sorts of images started running through my head at that moment. I didn't want to be around when my concerns became a reality.

I looked in the rearview and the cars were following us. I looked over to Jay and told him that we were being followed. He didn't seem as concerned as I was, which made me a little annoyed. I wasn't sure who these people were and what they wanted, nor did I want to find out. It was late and we should have just gone straight home. Even as I was thinking this, I looked back at the cars and noticed that the one directly behind us had a roof rack. I mention this to my friend. He looked over his shoulder and remarked that it wasn't a roof rack, but the lights of a police car.

This made me even more nervous. *But why? Why would they be following me? What had I done? I hadn't broken any laws. I couldn't have been speeding. There was nothing wrong with my truck.* I thought about every possible reason as to why they could possibly be following me and nothing came to mind. There was nothing that came to mind that would have prompted them to take up pursuit behind us. Nothing.

They stayed behind me as I approached the intersection that led out of the subdivision. I checked everything that I was doing and everything that they were doing to ensure that they wouldn't have cause to pull us over in the event they didn't already have one.

As I came to a full stop at the exit, I hit the turn signal, further ensuring the probability that there was nothing to worry about from the police. As we pulled out of the entrance, all I could see were flashing lights. We were being… I was being pulled over.

My heart was in my throat. I couldn't breathe. I kept running through my mind every possible thing that I might have done wrong and why we… I was being pulled over.

The officer pointed a blinding spotlight from his cruiser at my truck before getting out which left me only being able to see a silhouette as he approached. I could see him get out of car and begin walking up to my vehicle. As he did so, it felt like an eternity. All I heard were footsteps and the beating of my heart which was getting faster and faster. I could hardly see anything at all because of the beams of light emanating from his patrol car and the flashlight he was pointing in my direction. Before I knew it, he was at my side of the vehicle.

The officer came to my side and asked for the usual information: Driver's license, Insurance, Registration. As I handed him my documents, he started his interrogation.

"What are you doing out here tonight?"

He didn't ask or tell me of any infraction that I had committed. There was no reason that he had from my perspective to pull me over.

"I am just leaving work with my friend."

As he "inspected" me, his face demonstrated annoyance as he saw that I was wearing nothing to indicate I had just left any job that would have me out at that time. I was in jeans and a t-shirt that I changed into while waiting for my friend to get off. I often brought a change of clothes since I hated wearing a uniform when not working. I thought to myself that he is not going to believe me as I am sitting here dressed the way that I was.

The entire time that he was talking to me and looking me over with his flashlight, I could see that there was a second set of lights behind his vehicle. The other officer's cruiser had pulled behind this one's vehicle.

Am I that much of a threat? What had I done? I am just a teenage kid trying to drive through this neighborhood on the way to dropping off my friend after work. Two cop cars? I could be home by now… I have done nothing… nothing…

The officer still hadn't even looked at the information I had handed him. He looked over to Jay who still had his uniform and hat on. He couldn't look more relaxed. I still had my hands on the wheel at the "ten and two" position only to remove them in order to hand my information to the officer. He was laid back on the bench seat with one foot on my dash and a toothpick dangling from his mouth. In my head, I am calculating all the possibilities of us going to jail and the "charges" that this officer would come up with in order to take me in over and this asshole was sitting here without a care in the world. His relaxed demeanor was pissing me off more and more as each second passed.

"Is that true? Are you guys coming from work" asked the officer.

"Yeah," He replied.

"Yes, sir… we both are." I grabbed my hat off of my side of the dash to try and show it to him out of frustration.

Hesitantly, the officer handed me my paperwork and told us to be on our way. As we rode off, I watched every light, I came to a complete stop at every sign, and paid attention to the speed limit as was posted until I dropped Jay off.

When we arrived at his house his mother seemed a little concerned that we were arriving so late. With very little prodding, my friend revealed what had happened. I felt that, given what had taken place and what probably faced me when I got home, Jay was a little too forthcoming in letting his own mother know about us getting stopped by the police.

"What did you two do?"

Why was there the assumption that we had done anything wrong?

"Nothing. He just pulled us over," Jay answered.

"Well, did you get a ticket?" turning to me.

"No."

"Did you get a warning?"

"No." I was not in the mood to talk. I was still processing what had taken place. Jay's mother was all too confused at the fact that we had been stopped and released. She felt that there was something more that we were holding back, but knowing me, she knew that I wasn't one for trouble and wouldn't have done anything to prompt the police to pull us over.

When I listened to him discuss the events of the evening, I had little to offer as I was still trying to process it all. Unfortunately, it was one part of his story that hit me especially hard. He said something that really made me feel alone and really small. When his mother asked more about what took place, he joked about it. He minimized the situation. He turned my reality and safety into a point of ridicule.

Jay turned to his mom and chuckled, "He only let us off because he saw I was white." It wasn't a laughing matter to me. There was nothing humorous about the incident.

I did not want to believe it, but I had been in the car when it took place. I experienced what had happened and how the cop had reacted differently to the two of us. It hurt to the bone. He was right. I only thought about what may have occurred if I had been by myself when I was pulled over. If I had been alone, would there have been the same type of interaction and outcome?

I drove home feeling even lonelier than I had been in the car and in my friend's home earlier. The entire trip was a haze in that I could not picture any of the roads, cars, or anything that was on the route back to my house. The only thing that was on my mind was the incident that had happened roughly an hour earlier and the reality that my friend brought forth that I did not want to be true.

The more I thought about it, the more the reality sunk in. There was no disputing what had happened. The officer had pulled me over and not once during the stop did he state why he had done so. There were no curfew laws at the time in which we were breaking. I wasn't speeding, nor had I made any illegal turns or actions with my vehicle. Everything about the truck was in working order. The officer was looking for a reason to validate his stop when he had us pulled over. In the time that he had me stopped, he never returned to his vehicle to run my license or information. He never radioed his dispatcher or the other officer while by my vehicle. He spent his time trying to find something in my vehicle from a visual search to give him enough reason to escalate the situation. It wasn't until my friend was acknowledged that the situation changed. I thought about how much differently the circumstances would have been had he not been in the car with me that night.

When I walked into my house, no one was there waiting to scold me about being late or not having called for being delayed. Even if my mother had been waiting for my arrival, I would have been too humiliated to have discussed with her what had occurred. What took place, as menial as it may have seemed to some people brought to light that the idea of America and what I was being taught and raised to believe was not so. The idea that this nation is one in which everyone is to be treated equal and judged by the content of their character was flawed. I was angry. I was disappointed. I was ashamed. I felt alone and in a place where no one could understand and many aren't willing to comprehend.

Race Card

Ok… What are these things? Where can I get one? I have heard about the fabled "Race Card" for years and I have been jealous to the point that I have wanted one on my person to carry in instances of racial transgression. The problem is that no such thing exists. They are kind of like unicorns, dragons, or dilithium crystals.

It's an imaginary device that you have heard so many people make reference to routinely when they are uncomfortable with someone bringing issues of systemic racism and discrimination to their attention. If "Race Cards" were real, minorities would be unstoppable if we were actually in possession of them. I would pull one out like a soccer referee.

"The Race Card" has been referenced in so many issues and situations over the years it has me convinced that one must exist somewhere, so personally I will keep searching. Funny thing is, if people keep complaining about the "Race Card," doesn't that validate the existence of racism?

Making reference to the "Race Card" in a discussion about race does not remove the element of race from the issue, it only exacerbates it. It magnifies it. It doesn't give me admission to some secret club. It doesn't ensure that I have an easier life. I don't get special three-fifths discount or access to "special" items when out shopping.

Your reference to this imaginary item belittles this person's actual struggle with a social ill. If there were an actual "Race Card," I am sure that this person you were accusing of using it would have made the situation that brought them harm go away in the first place and would not have bothered you with their less than unpleasant experience. Besides, how do I keep getting this card when I am not even in control of the deck?

Chicken and Watermelon

"He's doing quite well, pretty impressive. That little boy is driving well and he's putting well. He's doing everything it takes to win. So, you know what you guys do when he gets in here? You pat him on the back and say congratulations and enjoy it and tell him not to serve fried chicken next year. Got it?... or collard greens or whatever the hell they serve." (Zoeller, 1997)

We get it, black people love fried chicken. It's an old trope, and stereotype, but everyone loves fried chicken. The problem with the fried chicken link to black people, other than the racial link, is the lack of style with the joke and humor. There has been no growth or development with it. Do people still tell Polish or Irish jokes on the regular?

The thing that is even more bothersome about the fried chicken line isn't that it is still around, but that it lacks any originality or imagination. People like to tell the joke or make the link as though they are the first one to make that correlation. It is almost as though they are some comedic sociologist enlightening the world with this discovery and smiling with glee that their thesis has been proven correct when they see some black folks in public enjoying a meal. When you do try to link this food or proclivity of one race to this food, you are being ignorant whether you want to admit it or not.

You can make the empty platitude of "well, everyone loves chicken" if you choose, but if the intent was to make a dig at one particular race or ethnicity because of a tired, old, worn out oversimplification, then you might need to rethink the intent. Although your goal may be intended to gain some camaraderie or a couple of chuckles, you may wind up demeaning and dehumanizing someone else in the process. The same goes for watermelon. And yes… I know. "Everyone" loves watermelon.

"JUMPING THE BROOM"

When it comes to weddings, very few guys put much thought into the event other than where they need to be and what time to be there. It isn't "our day." It is the bride's special day and is treated accordingly. The day that I exchanged vows with my then wife, my only concern was that my family attending from out of town felt welcome and enjoyed themselves during their visit.

The day of my wedding all of the last-minute adjustments had been made and bits of advice had been given from my parents to me about how life, marriage, and "going forward." There were no reservations expressed about the forthcoming nuptials. The photographers, wedding planner, and officiant were shocked at the relative calm.

My wife and I exchanged our vows and proceeded to the main hall for the reception. We made the rounds thanking people for their attendance, took pictures with friends and family, and exchanged pleasantries. There was no sense of tension in the air. Everything was as one should expect for their wedding day. Toasts were made and heartfelt, humorous speeches were delivered in order to commemorate the occasion. Everyone in attendance seemed to enjoy themselves. I never considered my identity to be a problem or a point of contention. As I looked around the room, I saw people of various color, faith, background, nationality, and profession. The event was the picture of diversity. This is what I often looked to when I thought a diverse, pluralistic society would look like. Everyone was enjoying themselves. It was too good to be true.

I reflected on the night and how things seemed to go so right. There was no air of discontent, at least not presented to me.

Days passed since vows were exchanged and my wife felt compelled to reveal something to me about the night that she herself was struggling with.

"Something happened at the wedding and I don't know what...well... I don't know what to think about it."

I was curious at this moment as to what was consuming her. She seemed more than a little occupied with an event that, from my estimation, occurred without incident.

"What is it?"

"Someone came up to my father during the reception and said that they were surprised that he was allowing his daughter to marry a black guy."

"Really?"

"They said 'I can't believe *you* are letting your daughter marry a black guy."

I was intrigued in that I was not surprised by someone having this type of opinion or mindset, but I was a little disturbed that they would bring it up at the wedding reception to her father.

"Well, what did he say to them?"

"Nothing. He just said that he wasn't going to discuss that there and walked away."

"That's it?"

"I think it was one of my aunts who said it. I am so pissed off. How could they say that to my Dad?"

"So, someone walked up to your father, said this, and he just brushed it off?"

"I overheard it, but I couldn't tell who it was. When I asked him about it, he changed the subject. I am pretty sure it was one of my aunts who said it. None of his friends would say something like that to him. I don't think anyone from my mom's family would have approached him."

I found myself trying to excuse why and how I should have defied their personal prejudices. "This is ridiculous. It's 2009. I have a good job, I'm not a criminal, I'm educated, I'm financially secure, but the only thing that they were concerned with is the color of my skin?"

She had missed the words and concern that had come out of my mouth.

"If I find out who it was, I am never talking to them again."

"And you father said nothing?"

"No, why?

"Because his silence speaks volumes on this issue."

She seemed confused on the whole situation. Her anger had been directed toward the individual making the initial comment to her father and wanted me to be equally angry about it. I had grown accustomed to people being uncomfortable with the idea of interracial relationships.

Growing up in the South, it was a pretty common mentality that people suffered from. There was this consistent fear that their daughter would end up with a "black guy" or wind up getting knocked up and having to support their biracial kid without the father being present. One of my roommates in college and a few people I worked with revealed to me that they wouldn't even date a girl if they found out that she had gone out with a black guy. That was the mindset in the South. There was some taint, some stain put on a woman the moment that she was associated with "a black guy." At a certain point, I just became numb to the entire narrative. What I was always curious about was what drove their rationale. What drove that fear? Why would it even be necessary to hold on to that mindset?

There have been interracial relationships, although not always legally recognized, in this nation for generations. In 1967, as a result of the Supreme Court's decision regarding *Loving v Virginia,* all bans regarding interracial relationships were deemed unconstitutional. Despite this legal ruling, there was still the social stigma which affected people's employment, housing, and family dynamics. The legality of their relationship did not remove the discrimination that they would face socially and professionally. Regardless of the ruling in *Loving v Virginia,* many people's perceptions had not progressed to see a couple as a couple, rather than an interracial couple which gave them the right to judge that their relationship was somehow deficient or invalid.

With my now former father-in-law, his silence in not addressing the individual who approached him signified to me that he himself had the same reservations about me taking his daughter's hand in marriage. Despite going through the same battle a generation earlier as an Hispanic man marrying a white woman in the late 1970s American Southwest. His in-laws brought forth the same objections directly to him, yet when the time came, he was not there to defend a man that was now a victim of that same ignorance and bigotry that he had faced thirty years prior. He did not have to have the person removed from the ceremony or even take up an aggressive approach. All he needed to do was to repeat the same encouraging words that he had said to me countless times where he referred to me as part of his family. He didn't. He listened to the ignorance. More importantly, this person felt comfortable enough with him to make this statement. They knew how he felt and that he would more than likely not protest what was to be said.

The statement itself was indicative of this. They were "surprised that he would allow" this to take place as though all of this was somehow secretly under protest. Any conversations that we had about how much he accepted me and any interactions prior to this incident was now hollow and any interactions since that day carried little weight due to his inability to address the comments of the person who made them. He never addressed them with his daughter and he never addressed them with me. Despite me being his son-in-law at the time and the man that he was trusting with his daughter's hand in marriage, the concern for him, for those in his own family, was not that I would be a good provider, hard worker, educated, or financially stable. Their concern was what color I was on the outside. To them and for so many people, this was a disqualifier for a relationship. It would always remain as a cloud over our relationship. This was not a situation that was limited to me. I was not the first, nor am I the last. Perhaps, one day, it won't even be a concern.

Cultural Navigations and Appropriations

Working as a lab technician for the Foreign Language department put me into contact with a variety of professors and instructors. I was able to engage them and learn more about their respective cultures, language, and their experiences in America. From time to time, through our mini cultural exchanges, they would ask me about aspects of American culture. I tried my best to clear up some of the confusion and answer their questions.

Dr O. had been in the country for only a few years and just joined our university in order to teach Japanese. He was always curious about American culture and trying to learn more about what it was that made us who we were. He wanted to know and learn as much as he could so that he could easily assimilate and avoid many of the social awkwardness that many immigrants had experienced. Dr. O. approached me looking very puzzled.

"Don, I have a question."

"Sure."
"What is it about Elvis?"

I cringed as I was unsure of where it was going,

but I had very little interest in discussing Elvis due to so many directions that it could head. I hated nearly everything about Elvis. I never understood the fascination with him and the devotion that many of his fans who, decades later, were still convinced of his infallibility and greatness. I felt, from his tone of curiosity, that he might be probing me to discuss the merits of his music and career. We were in the South and Elvis was a God here. Saying anything bad about Elvis is worse than proclaiming your hatred for Coca-Cola, Walmart, and Waffle House. He is not someone that you should disparage. People would disown their children for saying an unflattering word about "The King."

"What do you mean?"

"Well… In all of his songs he tries to sound like a black man with his tone and the slang. I thought that was bad. I thought that you weren't supposed to speak like that. Everyone tells me that this is the wrong way to speak, but this man is celebrated for singing his songs this way."

I tried as hard as I could to avoid the "black talk/white talk" conversation, but he persisted. I always thought that the "black/white" talk argument was crass and often a way in which to say that someone's speech was not dignified. With respect to his argument, he had a point, a valid one that had been made from time to time about Elvis. He made use of speech patterns that were somewhat "ethnic" in his music in order to capitalize on the lack of massive appeal that many black entertainers experienced.

"Not really. It's not that he is talking like he is black."

"No, Don. He's trying to be a black man. It's so obvious. Even I can see that and I don't speak the language."

Privilege

From time to time, my grandmother would share stories with me about growing up under Jim Crow. One that has always stood out to me involved her daily walk to school. We take this history for granted. When we often think about and discuss the Jim Crow era, we limit the scope to segregation and discrimination. It was much more than that. There were instances of violence to bodies and property. There was constant intimidation and harassment. America approved of and condoned tiered citizenship.

While I was still in college, she took the time to sit down with me and talk about how much had changed over her life. She mentioned how she was proud to have some of her children go to college and her pride grew even more to see her grandchildren with the opportunity to do even more. I never truly appreciated her sacrifice and struggle until she shared with me how deep the divide and hatred was for her and other black people as she grew up. Reflecting on the circumstances that she faced, I could never imagine having the strength that it would take to breathe, let alone live with the injustices that she, and many like her, faced.

When my grandmother Bernice was growing up, she had to deal with the reality of segregated schools, segregated facilities and a system that did not offer the same opportunities for her as white citizens. The school she attended had no heat in the winter. The roof leaked when it rained. There were hardly enough books for all of the students and the books that the school did have were in horrid condition. When it came to traveling to school, there was no transportation provided. All students going to the Negro schools had to walk. This was not the case for the white school in her area and the story that she lived mirrored that of many blacks growing up in the south during this period.

The concept of "separate but equal" was a fallacy. Everything was separate, while very little was equal. She saw the division and the way that her life and her people did not seem to matter. The daily trip to school cemented this reality. She and her friends would walk the dirt roads from their homes to the local school and each day the bus for the white school would pass them by. The students on the bus would mock them, laugh, make monkey noises, and call them "dirty niggers." They took the insults as the bus passed by and continued on to their destination each day. There was nothing they could do. They felt powerless, humiliated, dehumanized. This was their reality.

As the weeks passed, the white students on the bus understood the relationship that they had with the black students that they were passing and increased their levels of harassment. As my grandmother recounted, the bus would see them ahead on the road and would begin to slow down so the students on the bus could hurl more insults, and throw things at them as they made their way to school. She recalled how many of the students would even spit on them before the bus would continue on to its destination. There was little that they could do. They were in a situation that did not afford them the ability to fight back. They had no power. They were poor and black in the south.

As the harassment continued, the frustration built within my grandmother and a few of her friends who traveled on the route. They had devised a plan, if successful, that would result in their aggressors abandoning any future assaults. They were hoping to make a stand and demonstrate that they would not tolerated being treated as subhuman. They didn't consider the consequences, only the reward of being able to walk down that road in peace.

My grandmother and her schoolmates began their trek to school with the mindset that today would be the day that they took a stand. There was no more room to continue taking the abuse of these other children who they saw as having so many advantages over them and treated them so poorly only because of the tone of their skin. The bus approached to their rear and as it came over the horizon, the group began to get anxious about what they were about to do. Any and all resistance to the system in place could be met with extreme responses.

The bus approached them and as it came closer, they doubted themselves and what they were about to do. The bus slowed as it had in the previous meetings. Anxiety started to build in each of them. My grandmother and her friends turned to face their attackers. The students on the bus were excited to have another chance to spit on these "poor niggers." They rushed to let their windows down in order to lean their heads out ensuring that they didn't miss any of them as they passed. In their excitement, they did not notice the burlap sacks that each of these children were carrying with them.

As the children on the bus let down their windows in order to spit on these poor black children, all of those who were on the road launched the contents of their bags into the windows of the bus. Manure. The freshest horse, mule, and cow manure was now in the faces, hair, and mouths of nearly every white child who had attacked or attempted to attack them. In an instant, my grandmother and her friends realized what they had done and what this meant for their families. The bus came to a complete stop. All of the children on the bus were screaming, crying and cursing as a result of what had happened.

They ran. They ran into the fields. They ran into the woods. They ran into different directions. They just ran. They went in any and every direction that took them away from that road. They did not want to get caught by anyone on the bus or identified by the bus driver for their actions. They ran all the way to the school where they felt they would be safe. They understood that if they were seen sitting there, no one would suspect them as having anything to do with what took place with the "white folks' school bus."

They were anxious and on edge as they sat in their schoolhouse. What made them more anxious than their escape was the waiting. They waited for someone, anyone to burst through the door and arrest them, beat them, or worse. They worried that at any moment a white face would appear in that room and take them away with them never seeing their families again.

No one came by the school. As they walked home, no one was waiting for them on the road. Each step that they made, they expected someone to jump out in front of them to do harm. The journey seemed endless. As they arrived at their homes, there was no one there informing their parents of what they had done, nor evicting their parents from their tenant farms for this assault on southern pride and white dominance. They waited at their homes not telling their parents what had occurred earlier that day. They were scared of facing the punishment that would be doled out at home for stirring up trouble. Nothing happened that night. No one came by asking about what took place on that road. No retribution was committed to any blacks in the area. No one even made so much as a whisper about the incident. Nothing came of it that night. They couldn't explain to anyone what they had done. As proud as they were for standing up for themselves, they could not make mention of their actions.

The next day, my grandmother and her friends cautiously made their way to school down the same dirt road they had long traveled. They talked about the previous day's events and discussed the possibility of anyone knowing or talking about it, but they all had the same experience. None of their families knew nor did any of the neighbors. No one came looking for them. They continued walking the lonely dusty road, waiting for that bus to approach. They continuously looked over their shoulders while on their voyage, but nothing came. It wasn't until they had reached the school that they realized that the bus was not coming. When the time came to go home, the same thoughts had entered their minds, "Where is the bus? When is it coming? What are they going to do to us this time?" It never came.

When my grandmother told me this story, she was proud that she took a stand that day and unashamed in telling it. At the time that it happened, as she told me, there was fear, a deep fear and concern that at any moment someone would drag you out of your home in the middle of the night and kill you in any number of ways for lesser offenses. She was a child at this time, years before Emmett Till would be tortured and murdered in Mississippi for whistling at a white woman, but the reality of violence to uphold the social order was no stranger to rural Virginia. The fear for her was not that she would be whipped or punished for her actions that day, but she had witnessed racial violence inflicted on so many others already in her young life.

She feared that she or someone she knew would be found swinging from the end of a rope. She feared that her house or church might be burned down in the middle of the night. She feared that her school might be shot at or firebombed while it was in session.

Her fear was that she would not live to see adulthood because of someone else's choice to uphold the racial order. She feared that someone else had the power to take her life, property, or freedom without any justice being served on her behalf because they saw little value in her life. She was a human being, but there were people who did not and never would see her as such simply because of her skin color. This was her reality.

"What do you call a black guy with a Ph.D.?"

The English Historian, Lord Acton stated that the only true test of determining whether a nation was truly free was by observing how it treated its minorities. Their observations and perspectives allow for people to reflect on social injustice, inequality, and plight that have gone unsolved.

Within any society, people look for a balance between the pain and comfort. Comedians have long had the opportunity and potential to bring attention and greater focus to social ills. Some, have taken more active roles, choosing to address the issues directly so that their audiences are greater informed about the changes that need to be made. Other comedians pursued a more passive approach. Because of his more passive role, likeability, and even his ability to be accepted by mainstream America, Bill Cosby virtually became America's Token Black, while Dick Gregory became a polarizing figure due to his political and social views. The two strategies yielded different results for these performers' careers and lives. Dick Gregory and Bill Cosby are two prominent examples of this struggle between passive and active agents of change.

Mr. Gregory began his professional career in 1958 amid a changing American framework and society that seemed to be trying to find its own identity. Segregation was still a harsh reality within comedy and comedy clubs. Dick Gregory was not satisfied with this reality and began to use his comedy as a vehicle to tear down the walls that existed between people. In 1961, he began performing in Chicago at the Playboy Club. By choosing the wrong bus one night of a performance, he ended up being late for the set that he originally had.

When he arrived, he was told that he couldn't go out and perform because of the audience, which was comprised of many southern whites. He was not deterred. He knew how to handle a crowd and convinced his way onto the stage. He opened with jokes that reflected many of the social and racial attitudes that he felt this crowd might have. He also knew that he had to disarm them once he came onto the stage.

> Good evening ladies and gentlemen. I understand there are a good many southerners in the room tonight. I know the South very well. I spent twenty years there one night.
>
> Last time I was down South I walked into this restaurant and this white waitress came up to me and said, "We don't serve colored people here." I said, "That's all right. I don't

> eat colored people. Bring me a whole fried chicken"
>
> Then these three white boys came up to me and said, "Boy, we're givin' you fair warnin'. Anything you do to that chicken, we're gonna do to you." So I put down my knife and fork, I picked up that chicken and I kissed it. Then I said, "Line up, Boys!" (Weide)

From this performance, he was booked for a three-year run at the Playboy Club. Because of his rising prominence within comedy, he was invited to perform on the *Tonight Show.* At first, Gregory was hesitant to accept the offer. The entertainment industry, despite being seen as progressive, also mirrored some of the attitudes, perspectives, and behaviors of American society. There were segregated clubs throughout the North and the South. His reservations were reasonable because of the challenges that he faced while in college and the US ARMY. When he spoke with Jack Paar, the host of *The Tonight Show,* he made a simple request by today's standards: he wanted to sit on the couch. The reality of television and the way that people saw comics, actors, and performers of all kinds began to change with that simple request. His request was honored by the host himself. The reality that perceptions were changing was being brought forth because of a simple request by this one comedian from St. Louis. Gregory understood the request and its meaning. Just a few years earlier, many Southern NBC affiliates would not show the *Nat King Cole Show* because of its headliner and host who was Black. The restrictions put on race were restrictive for performers who wanted to break through and become available to mainstream audiences. After his performance on *The Tonight Show,* Paar invited him to sit on the couch, a major accomplishment by any comedian. Once you are invited to sit on the couch, it is symbolic that you have made it, you have met the approval of those who can affect the perceptions and misperceptions about who you are and those who look like you. This meant much to Gregory on the individual level, but it also reflected the way that America, as a whole, was becoming a much more socially conscious and an active participant in the movements that were transitioning attitudes of the 1950s into the 1960s.

Gregory gained success from that one night on television that made him recognizable and a highly-desired performer. For his regular stint at the Playboy Club, his pay had increased from $250 per week to $5000 a night. The previous year he had earned a total of $1500 by his own estimations. The appearance and the paycheck were not what gave Gregory pride. In one interview regarding the appearance on *The Tonight Show* he stated that being on the show and being able to sit on the couch made him feel as though he was actually in America, that he was, in fact, welcome. This dream of what America is or can be was something that he knew could be achieved if brought to the attention of America. It was something that had to be felt by everyone, not just those with money, or with the right skin tone. Gregory wanted all Americans to feel what he felt on that couch.

Gregory became more active in the Civil Rights movement of the 1960s. He would march throughout the south for voting rights and support groups such as the Student Non-violent Coordinating Committee (SNCC), the Southern Christian Leadership Committee (SCLC), and the National Association for the Advancement of Colored People (NAACP). Gregory actively participated in sit-ins, fundraisers, voter drives, and various protests. Because of his participation, Gregory began to turn down many of his normal gigs, many because he could not attend due to incarceration from his participation in the movements, others because he personally did not see the importance in performing in nightclubs anymore when there was much greater work to be accomplished. He had remarked in his later years that "The world have never liberated nobody through humor or through comedy. If they find a cure for cancer, it won't be through humor. All the gains that black people have made in America in the last thirty years, it wasn't through comedy, it wasn't through entertainment. It was through folks who we don't even know their name, that went out there and died on the frontlines" (Akwamu). When he went up on that stage, he went to get a laugh, not to change anyone's mind. He stated that when he went on marches, he didn't do so in order to get laughs. He saw that there was a marked difference between Dick Gregory the entertainer and Dick Gregory the Civil Rights Campaigner.

He knew that his celebrity brought attention to the causes he served, and that was the only purpose that it had for him. There was to be no joke telling or humor as part of his marches or movement to extend freedom to people throughout the nation, nor was he going to be able to use the nightclub to educate those that he needed to in order to bring about effective change to a system that was impacting so many.

Gregory understood the path that he was taking and that he was risking his career and life in order to proceed on this path. He stated that when he joined the movement in Mississippi, he joined knowing that he was going to die. Regardless of this possibility, and the reality that it happened to others, he went. His drive was knowing that death was not the worst thing that would come out of the movement. Growing up in segregated neighborhoods, he knew that a paycheck was not something that should be held over his head when it came time to account for what he had done with his life. Mr. Gregory understood that it would be disgraceful to walk away from the opportunity that he currently had as a participant in the Civil Rights Movement. The greater change that he would be able to bring forth would not be through his wallet, but through his voice as he had seen through his friends Dr. Martin Luther King, Jr., and Malcolm X. Others had died and would die during the course of the movement. By removing himself, he felt as though he was being tolerant of systemic racism and being accepting of it (Zaire). When he was confronted by a journalist about how the movement was impacting his career, Gregory replied that he had his information wrong. The reality was quite the opposite. It was his career that was getting in the way of his political activities (Krehbiel).

Much like Dick Gregory, Bill Cosby would bring about change through his comedy and celebrity. However, his method would take a more passive approach. After dropping out of high school in the tenth grade, Bill Cosby joined the NAVY and served as a hospital Corpsman. The experience of treating Korean War vets brought him to the realization of what was important. He understood the importance of an education and that it in liberating individuals and societies. He immediately finished the requirements to receive his equivalency diploma and earned a scholarship to Temple University based on his athletic ability from high school. He would bring about change in his own way.

Bill Cosby began his professional career at roughly the same time as Gregory. He began working in clubs throughout Philadelphia and then moved performance clubs like the Gaslight Café which afforded him the opportunity to have his comedy heard by a more diverse crowd earlier in his career than Gregory did. His exposure in venues like this built his reputation and eventually led to a performance on *The Tonight Show* in 1963.

Bill Cosby's style was one that reflected similarities, observations, reflections, and general humor. His was not a style that discussed race specifically or anything that seemed taboo for the time. He did not feel that was a way for him to engage his audiences or, in effect, be an agent of change to reform the image that some people may have of blacks in their minds. Through his humor, he would often remark that he felt that it was a way to create a bridge between black and white communities. The similarities seen within their daily lives would be important to create understanding of what was important. He was opposed to playing up the differences between white and black. He created a link and demonstrated the universal characteristics of black and white culture and livelihoods. This helped to create a bridge of understanding for mainstream America in gaining his personal perspective. As a young comic in the 1960s, Cosby said, he didn't want to be like other black comedians and talk about race issues. "I don't play that," he said. "You're not going to laugh at the color of my skin. You're going to laugh with me at our similarities, and some of our differences. But I'm not going to have you, because this is not the time in this United States of America, where you're going to laugh at what my people are suffering with" (*Jacksonville Free Press*).

Cosby's career was beginning to take off in 1965 with a lead role on the television show, *I Spy.* The role was groundbreaking. This opportunity brought him more exposure with a national audience. The afforded with the ability to reach an even wider public than with his performances in comedy clubs or his comedy albums.

Bill Cosby came under criticism for not taking an active role in the Civil Rights movement through marches, delivering speeches, attending rallies, or even providing his own commentary about what he deemed to be important, necessary changes to ensure equality and full citizenship. One could argue that doing so would negatively impact his career and marginalize him with his audiences. With Gregory, it was clear that the issue of race and aspects pertaining to it appealed to him. He was not concerned about the impact to his career. Gregory often remarked that he was an activist first and an entertainer second.

Cosby's appeal was that people found comfort in his comedy. Veering from this would change who he was as an entertainer and risk losing the mainstream appeal that he was gaining with his popularity. This was very instrumental as Bill Cosby returned to standup comedy in the 1970s. The style remained the same, yet his focus and humor engaged his audiences with the universal themes of marriage, family, and parenthood. These were not race specific issues. These were ways that, just in his early comedy and television career, he was able to break down barriers between black and white audiences.

When Cosby was given the opportunity to enter the realm of television again, it would be a show that was built around his comedy. *The Cosby Show* offered a sharp contrast to previous black family sitcoms like *Sanford and Son, and Good Times*. These shows came to unfortunately associate negative societal aspects with Black Culture for mainstream audiences. Instead of the show's basis being about poverty and plight, his new show featured a stable middle-class family structure. It offered a true representation of the Black middle class which had existed in America for generations. The problem was that there was no real exposure of this existence to mainstream America.

The Cosby Show presented to American

audiences a successful black family with Black consciousness and concerns in everyday Black life. *The Cosby Show* showcased a high level of positive images that were far ahead of other Black sitcoms. The Black style of the characters is evident in their speech, intonations and nuances. The show mentioned famous Black authors, and books. It showcased Black art, music and dance. It introduced America to Historically Black Colleges and Universities (HBCUs), and later through his spin-off *A Different World*.

Many argue that although *The Cosby Show* "attempts to break the chokehold of such traditional black stereotypes" it does not reflect the typical Black family or life. The domestic bliss of the Huxtable household is perceived by whites as the exception to the rule of black family life, reaffirming the notion that racism would not be a problem if only blacks were more like "us." Theories such as that only justify the racial stereotypes that exist in this country. Cosby's main goal was to eliminate stereotypes such as that one (Crenshaw). Claire Huxtable, Cosby's wife on the show did not storm in or behave in a boisterous comical way much like Aunt Esther or other female black characters had done in past televisions shows. Her refinement, her charm, and her attitude helped to bring to the attention of black and white audiences that Black culture and characterization is not something that can be defined by stereotypes, generalizations, and misperceptions.

Cosby was very clear of how he wanted the show to represent black people and black culture. He wanted a break from the past which had characterized black roles as being clowns, downtrodden and having very little class. Cosby sought to use this new platform to break down stereotypes about the Black Community and demonstrate the positive aspects that he felt were underrepresented in film and television. This was a strategy imposed not just for outside observers to have a better understanding of people who could be seen as different as themselves, but for the Black Community, as well. Civil Rights Legislation is one thing; however, it does little to have someone relate to your circumstances or for one who feels left out of the American Experience.

Throughout his career, Gregory's focus has been about taking his message to his audiences rather than allow for his message to speak for him. He became much more confrontational with his message and topics. To this day, he is not deterred from discussing topics that many have avoided.

Bill Cosby, in recent years, has become more vocal in his criticisms of Black Society, taking a tone that many were surprised to hear from him. He addressed an audience in Atlanta on the 50th anniversary of *Brown versus Board of Education:*

Brown Versus the Board of Education is no

longer the white person's problem. We've got to take the neighborhood back. We've got to go in there. Just forget telling your child to go to the Peace Corps. It's right around the corner. It's standing on the corner. It can't speak English. It doesn't want to speak English. I can't even talk the way these people talk. "Why you ain't where you is go, ra," I don't know who these people are. And I blamed the kid until I heard the mother talk. Then I heard the father talk. This is all in the house. You used to talk a certain way on the corner and you got into the house and switched to English. Everybody knows it's important to speak English except these knuckleheads. You can't land a plane with "why you ain't..." You can't be a doctor with that kind of crap coming out of your mouth. There is no Bible that has that kind of language. Where did these people get the idea that they're moving ahead on this? Well, they know they're not, they're just hanging out in the same place, five or six generations sitting in the projects when you're just supposed to stay there long enough to get a job and move out. We have to begin to build in the neighborhood, have restaurants, have cleaners, have pharmacies, have real estate, have medical buildings instead of trying to rob them all. And so, ladies and gentlemen, please, Dorothy Height, where ever she's sitting, she

> didn't do all that stuff so that she could hear somebody say "I can't stand algebra, I can't stand…and "what you is." It's horrible.
>
> Basketball players, multimillionaires can't write a paragraph. Football players, multimillionaires, can't read. Yes. Multimillionaires. Well, Brown V Board of Education, where are we today? It's there. They paved the way. What did we do with it? The white man, he's laughing, got to be laughing. 50 percent drop out, rest of them in prison. You got to tell me that if there was parenting, help me, if there was parenting, he wouldn't have picked up the Coca Cola bottle and walked out with it to get shot in the back of the head. He wouldn't have. Not if he loved his parents. And not if they were parenting! Not if the father would come home. Not if the boy hadn't dropped the sperm cell inside of the girl and the girl had said, "No, you have to come back here and be the father of this child." Not "I don't have to." (Cosby)

The words cut through his audience and made the nickname "America's Dad" become all too real. Bill Cosby had taken the time that he had built up his reputation to become a subtle subversive and try to change the consciousness of America and especially Black America as to their abilities, worth, and role. Now in his later years he has had the ability to take those credentials and trust that he built in being a mainstream figure and make people really think. If he had taken this approach earlier in his career, it may not have had the same reaction as it did on that day or the following speaking engagements and interviews where he repeated the stances that he took in front of that crowd in Atlanta.

The difference between Dick Gregory and Bill Cosby is that they had the same outlook to their activism as one might argue Dr. Martin Luther King, Jr. and Malcolm X had in their approaches. One would argue for passive resistance and non-violence, while the other would argue that they needed to be confrontational with their desires for change. Each achieved different results through their focus of action and this impacted them on a personal and professional level. Gregory left the nightclubs in order to become more active in social movements. In 1968 he ran for President on the Freedom and Peace Party as a write-in candidate. His popularity with mainstream audiences diminished over the years because of his political involvement and his focus on being more of an educator and activist rather than an entertainer. To this day, Gregory participates in protests, hunger strikes, and performs at various speaking engagements throughout the country to keep his audiences engaged and informed with the hope that they will think and ask questions. His son, when asked about his father's activities remarked that "Everything you hear, everything you heard him say… is him 365 days a year. He continues to carry the torch when so many have opted out" (Kirksey).

Bill Cosby's career flourished by taking a more passive role toward social issues and commentary. With *The Cosby Show* and its spinoff, *A Different World,* he had two network hits that helped shaped the image and perception of African-Americans. He received much criticism for not taking an active role early in his career and a fair amount for his critique of Black Society later in life. He was able to have a greater impact through the ability to change people's vision and to provide people with a vision. Despite the criticism, he understood that his goal was inspire others.

Despite taking different routes to push for change, both men made significant impacts within society. It is clear that Dick Gregory's career suffered because of his political activity and focus on social issues, however, Dick Gregory would argue that his work never suffered because his main passion was social issues and pushing for change. Gregory states that the most important thing is that you understand who you are and what your spirit is about (Bayliss). They both understood their spirit and their purpose. Because of this, they were both able to change people's minds, perceptions, and realities without losing who they are and what they stand for.

Growing up, Bill Cosby and his TV persona, Dr Cliff Huxtable, were the authority on fatherhood and he was someone that everyone could relate with despite race, income, or social background. He was given the title of "America's dad." Not "America's Black Dad," but "America's Dad." He and his message were accepted by mainstream America… or so I thought.

During my freshman year of high school, I received a "revelation" from one of my teachers. While discussing influences, role models, etc., Bill Cosby was brought up. With it being the mid-1990s, and the *The Cosby Show* having been on the air for quite a while, it had long cemented its status as part of the American landscape and pop culture. It was at this moment that my teacher, someone whom I had come to trust and admire, lost all credibility with me.

When discussing the merits of *The Cosby Show* and even getting into its spinoff, *A Different World*, she stated, "That show is a fantasy. The father is a doctor and the mother is a lawyer. Black people don't really live like that." There were only 3 black students in the room, but even at the time, I thought about how bold and damaging a statement like this was. You are telling a generation of people that there is no one of their background, no one that looks like them could possibly live as well as, be as educated as, sophisticated as, or as accomplished as the Huxtables. Worse yet, she was voicing this to a majority white audience who would parrot the same message and believe the idea that black people could not hold the possibility of this existence. It continued the distortion that their peers of color were destined to live in degradation, squalor, ghettos, or projects much like they would see throughout popular media.

The topic of *The Cosby Show* resurfaced while I was working in college. One of my coworkers was complaining about how there wasn't anything good on television anymore. She began to rail off some shows that she used to grow up with and *Cosby* happened to be one of them. I assumed that the discussion was heading in a direction that would follow her line of thinking. I was proven wrong. As she began to reminisce about the shows she loved and the time she spent watching it with her family members she became familiar enough with me to share an experience from her youth. She recalled her grandmother calling her into the family room when the *Cosby Show* was about to come on.

"Y'all hurry up and get in here. *The Niggers* is about to come on!"

She chuckled as she said it not in recognition of

her grandmother's ignorance, but in reminiscing about that moment. It seemed nostalgic to her. It was actually funny that her grandmother was calling the show "The Niggers." She said it with a smile on her face. She didn't see the remark as something to be ashamed of or provide any distance between herself and the statement. It was acceptable. When I questioned her as to why she found this funny, she was oblivious. She just found it funny to refer to the show as "The Niggers," as well. I was a bit blown away and befuddled by her demeanor and pride at this memory. I was just as surprised at her ability to be so clueless about the offense.

I grew frustrated and began discussing not only the history of the show with her, but Cosby's personal story and accomplishments, as well. For that moment, it was imperative that there was an explanation of how the show helped to redefine images of black people in popular media and America, in general. She didn't seem to get where I was coming from with my disgust over her lighthearted approach to her and her family's degradation of this program and its legacy. For her family, who had grown up in the rural south, in poverty, there was one thing that made them different or stand out from Cosby, at least in their eyes. They might be poor, but they weren't niggers. These were the kind of people who fit perfectly in Nixon's "Southern Strategy," following the same logic set forth by Lyndon Johnson that the lowest white man can be convinced that they are better than the best black man. No matter the accomplishments of this or any other person of color in her grandmother's eyes, what mattered more to them was on the outside and the social order and hierarchy surrounding that. They weren't niggers. That was all that mattered. This is a point of emphasis that had been handed down for generations and further shaped their views and perspectives solidifying Jim Crow, tracking programs, redlining, restrictive covenant contracts, racial violence, and discrimination and bigotry at all levels. In that moment, it became even more clear to me what the true reality was behind a punch line to a horrible joke I had heard too many times when I was younger.

Out of anger, annoyance, frustration, and a bit of bitterness, I ended the conversation. Before walking away from her, I asked one question that left her puzzled. "What do you call a black guy with a PhD?"

WWMLKS?

Whether it was the LA riots, the recent unrest Baltimore, Ferguson, Florida, Cleveland, Chicago, or any time in which African-Americans take to the streets to show their frustration with the criminal justice system, public education, social strife, disenfranchisement, police brutality, or political corruption, the chorus coming from mainstream America in response to their actions is a steady stream of "What would Martin Luther King say about this?"

For starters, he'd probably say to stop invoking his name, likeness, image, words, and taking his speeches out of context with respect to every situation you find yourself faced. Likewise, he would understand how he was being used by people in order to absolve themselves of any social responsibility in actually addressing the issues that have led to the protests and riots. Dr. King, might not be focused on about what he had to say, but what he could do in order to help alleviate many of the social ills in those areas. He would march, protest, and boycott in order to help bring about change. In doing so, he would be criticized by the same groups of people who want to put him up on a pedestal while wiping their boots on those who have concerns in the here and now. In fact, he would be doing much of what current civil rights groups, organizations, and social activists are participating in today.

The crowds of detractors who are invoking the spirit and legacy of Dr. King are cut from the same cloth as those who referred to him as a troublemaker, race baiter, hustler, communist, and any number of other denigrating and disparaging terms when he himself was fighting for equal rights, access to voting, political rights, economic independence, social justice and basic human dignity. It is convenient to exploit his words or memory to criticize and chastise current movements, while ignoring his actions in order to correct current conditions or even investigate their circumstances.

Why even resort to mentioning MLK's words? Is this meant to serve as a pacifying effect for the black community whenever there is a moment of discord? Is this somehow going to serve as the conscience for African-Americans to where the very mention of Dr. King will make us in unison and in lock-step join together and think, "You're right. What was I thinking?" as if their "Dr. King chip" is activated and we regain our senses.

Dr. King is not a fail-safe option with respect to a group and race of people that can be used at will whenever any number of that group are suffering or expressing their outrage. This invocation of MLK by mainstream America is grounded in a need to make themselves feel good and appear enlightened. Of course, it relies on much erasure about the history and politics of the 1950s and 1960s, as well as, an erasure of Dr. King, himself.

Utilizing him and his spirit is disingenuous. Is Dr. King the go-to because he is a voice of reason or is he the go-to because he is the only relatable black voice of reason that people choose to look to in moments like these? If the latter is the case, it is a disservice to his legacy in that only applying his words to the actions of black people runs counter to what the man stood for. He pushed for equal opportunity and equal treatment across color lines. His advice was not for Black people, but for the American people as a whole. His messages brought to the national dialogue the social ills that the black and the poor bore witness to on a daily basis. If anything, he served as a conscience for all Americans.

His statements, advice, speeches, warnings, and words were not limited in scope to the time and circumstances in which he lived. It further demonstrates the lack of understanding that mainstream America and the media have about Black people in general. It also signifies that this is the only black person that they are familiar with and comfortable using in relation to the Civil Rights movement as a transformative figure. In doing so, they affirm that Dr. Martin Luther King, Jr. is America's Token Black Civil Rights Icon despite the numerous individuals who existed before him in the movement, influenced him, those who stood beside him during the height of the 1950s and 1960s and those who helped to continue the fight forward.

There were individuals who made statements just as profound and defining as he did in the realm of music, poetry, journalism, labor movements, political movements, social progress, and the Civil Rights era, but they are often overlooked because of the focus that we have collectively paid toward Dr. King.

Dr. King was a transformative figure and his contributions will stand the test of time as we move forward as a nation. What doesn't help the dialogue is the constant referencing of MLK as if he were the omnipresent soul of Black America and the voice of reason that we need to be reminded of. This is counter-productive and runs in contrast to what the man stood for. The use of MLK allows those using him to remove themselves from the discussion. It is a simplistic response to very complex situations.

Dr. King isn't here to give his opinions. He isn't here to offer advice. He had offered his advice before. He had counseled politicians and communities as to what could be done. The groups moving forward are part of his legacy and those who marched and fought alongside him.

Quoting Dr. King and bringing him into the discussion to condemn current political movements and social unrest serves as nothing more than an empty platitude. It is a disregard for the reality of the situations at hand and the ability of those witnessing the circumstances to actually turn their back on it by offering nothing more than an admonishment of what they themselves cannot and possibly do not wish to understand. It is a way of exposing how people are not mature enough or even willing to deal with current circumstances.

They don't want to leave their comfort zone in order to focus on the ugly realities that many communities face, nor are they willing to lift a hand for that cause other than to wag a finger. They want to sit on the sidelines and complain about those trying to exercise their rights of protest and political action in response to injustices. They are comfortable and complacent with the way the world works for them. They seem to have forgotten the words of the man they so desperately want to invoke when it fits their narrative or rose-colored sense of existence: "Injustice anywhere is a threat to justice everywhere." Perhaps they should consider his thought that "Our lives begin to end the day we become silent about things that matter." Then again, maybe if there is this desperation to point to a leader of color as the voice in quelling a populace, they might want to consider the words of Bishop Desmond

Tutu that "If you are neutral in situations of injustice, you have chosen the side of the oppressor. If an elephant has its foot on the tail of a mouse and you say that you are neutral, the mouse will not appreciate your neutrality."

Instead of wagging fingers and admonishing people for responses to their situations, it would be beneficial to try and understand their pain, their frustration, and their circumstances. It is essential that you understand before you can disagree. You will able to see what can be done to help instead of deferring to Dr. King and demonstrating that you view him as nothing more than a Token Black Martyr.

Southern Heritage

I always found the wearing and flying of the Confederate Battle flag confusing and perplexing. It always seemed to me as something of a relic and an item that didn't belong in the public space considering its sordid history and association with not only the Civil War, but with the Jim Crow Era, as well. I spent the majority of my life in the south where, at times, it could often be seen flying more than the flag representing the nation that we were all living in. I had friends and classmates in high school who wore clothing with the emblem on it. Hardly a day went by where I didn't sit in traffic next to someone who had some representation of the "Stars and Bars" on their vehicle.

At a certain point, you think that someone would get used to seeing things like this or even become numb to it. I never got used to it. I was unwilling to accept the skewed reality its followers accepted as fact or found comforting about it. I never wanted to become used to it. Becoming used to it would mean that I accepted it and became complicit in this practice. It always seemed abnormal to me. It always made me question the rationale as to why people thought that this symbol was one in which to rally around and one in which to associate their heritage.

I didn't like engaging people about this issue too often. It was my feeling at the time that if they were happy living in denial, I wasn't going to be able to break them from their ignorance by shining a light on it. One such moment found me when I was sixteen.

Timberland boots were in style and were quickly becoming synonymous with Hip-Hop. I wanted a pair but lacked the funds and was willing to settle for a pair that looked similar to them. A friend suggested stopping by one of the local Army Surplus shops. Convinced that I would find a pair for a reasonable price, I stopped by after school. The store was full of all of the general wares that one would expect; camo, guns, camping gear, etc. Being a military kid I was somewhat fascinated by all of the different items. I was impressed with the amount of inventory in a store that seemed quite small. The store was empty of people aside from myself and two individuals who appeared to run the place; a middle-aged male wearing a ball cap and a woman of about the same age with dark hair. They were carrying on a seemingly meaningless conversation while I looked around. I perused the shelves and found all types of items before coming across the boots. As I looked them over trying to find my size, I heard a voice from behind the counter.

"Hey, tell me… You're a young black man."

This isn't going to be good…

"What do you think about that flag? What does that mean to you?" asked the woman as she was pointing to a 3′x5′ Confederate flag that was hanging over the counter.

I was taken aback at the way she abruptly asked me to engage in some sort of discourse about the Confederate Battle Flag. The store felt even smaller than when I had entered as I was now on the spot as to my personal views on a piece of inflammatory cloth. It was just the three of us. There was no significant moment on my part which initiated the necessity for a discussion about race or this flag altogether.

The only response I had for her question was abrupt.

"Nothing. It doesn't mean anything to me."

"See, I told you," she said turning back to her

friend. The air that had carried my words had barely reached her by the time that she responded.

She was so focused on what she saw the flag as to not consider the meaning behind what I had said, nor did she ask for clarification. To be honest, I don't think that staying in that shop and explaining myself any further would have changed her perception about the flag. While she was so consumed with glee that a young black man had "agreed" with her stance in supporting the confederate flag, I walked out of the store so I would not find myself in any "deeper" social commentary.

The reality is that she may not have cared about my opinion other than for it to validate the one that she already held. She was looking for confirmation, someone who would agree with her on this issue. She wasn't prepared to argue about how this flag somehow represented heritage or the history that she saw in the flag. Her perspective was one that I ran into countless times. It was one in which she wanted to show her pride in wearing or flying the confederate flag and "if you are offended by it, well, then it's your problem."

The truth is I hate that flag. I hate everything about it. I hate its history. I hate the way in which it is revered throughout the South as if it were a holy artifact that must be worshipped each and every chance one gets. What I hate most are the excuses and rationale that people give to why they wear it, why they fly it, why they permit it to become ubiquitous and run from any conversation that attempts to dismantle the myth that has become linked to it. I despise the imagery. I detest and refute the lie that people have convinced themselves of that it represents some noble cause that their ancestors fought and died for. This is exactly what I meant by it meaning nothing to me. It has no substance and no real meaning.

The problem is that people continue on with this lie that the flag is cloaked in honor. The Confederacy itself was built off of the subjugation of another race. It was the basis in which the Confederacy used to galvanize support throughout the south. All of the arguments that are brought forth in which people claim it is not about hate, rather it is about their history or heritage, the question then becomes, what is that history and heritage built upon? What is that flag representative of if nothing more than a league of people who were seeking the continued subjugation of another race of people?

Southerners love fantasy. They love the

romanticized history brought to life in the figures of Rhett Butler and Scarlet O'Hara. They love this lie that they retell it year after year. We never want to see ourselves as who we truly are. We want to be the protagonist. We want to be the hero in the white hat riding in on his stallion to save the day. It is hard to come to terms with the fact that one's heritage is built off of being the villain. No one wants their legacy to be defined as being on the wrong side of history. Coming to terms with that reality is too much for many to bear. People love fantasy.

The confederate flag is not the reason why Jim Crow legislation, Racial Violence, Segregation, Race Riots, prejudice, and racism existed. It didn't commit the heinous lynchings of countless men, women and children. It isn't responsible for the torture and brutal murder of Emmett Till. The Confederate Flag did not bomb the Ebenezer Street Baptist Church. The Confederate Flag did not riot over James Meredith, The Little Rock Nine, or Ruby Bridges being admitted to their first days of school and breaking the "color barrier" for their respective institutions. It represents that hate, the seething anger held within the hearts and minds of those men and women who would pull out their banners in response to their societal norms, customs, and social order being changed. It symbolizes all the actions by those people who committed them and those who condoned them because they felt that they were justified in doing so by standing up for the "Southern Way of Life."

Flying this flag over state capitols and municipal buildings helped to create and cement this false reality and reminds people of this tainted heritage and history, but not in the proper context. People of all colors should be ashamed, embarrassed, and appalled that this banner and any version derived from it or similar to it was allowed to fly one day past April 9th of 1865. Having the Confederate flag in our public spaces and a continuance of the Southern Heritage lore allows for generations of Americans, not just Southerners, to swim in seas of ignorance and racial tensions.

When the "Southern Heritage" narrative is brought into the conversation we have to admit that it is a fabrication of the truth. It omits many of the circumstances surrounding the period in which that "Heritage" builds its pride off of. Those who tout the "Southern Pride" or "Southern Heritage" argument as reasoning for not pushing forth with change in the South are doing nothing more than keeping the ghosts of the past alive. They are keeping the flames of Margaret Mitchell, D.W. Griffith, and William Dunning burning. The Confederacy was built on racial supremacy and hatred. It survives on fears and falsehoods.

The cold reality is that many of those who continue flying the flag or wearing it on their garments don't want to come to terms with what it actually represents. They want to control the narrative and want the general public to accept this definition and to accept this false reality being pushed in order for it to become the accepted reality for everyone. No one wants to be the villain. No one wants to be associated with the tainted legacy of American history in which we see images of George Wallace standing in the doorway of the University of Alabama.

This symbol becomes emblematic for so many. It is a roadblock, a barrier, and an obstacle to social and political progress. It is a sign which lets others know, "you're not welcome." There is no ownership of the history other than "heritage." There is no acceptance or acknowledgment of the injustices that were committed under that banner that is waved or worn. Although one might not be condoning the actions of the past, their lack of being honest about it does little to create a break from that negative image. America is about a continuous movement toward progress, change, and inclusion. The same cannot be said about the Confederacy, Confederate sympathizers, or Confederate flag.

When you fly that flag, it signifies that you don't want to be part of America. It signifies that you don't want to move forward. The desire to hold on to this piece of the past is done so with a close-minded approach and one that is wholly limited and peppered with exclusion. Supporters don't want to join the rest of us beyond the 19th century and ensure that people of all races, creeds, colors, religions and genders have their rights protected under the Constitution. What it signifies is that you truly yearn for the days in which thirteen states broke off from the Union in order to lay claim to their own sovereign nation built on the ideals of inequality. One can argue about their heritage, about their history and how their waving or wearing of the "stars and bars" is not about racism, what they cannot say is that it is about is patriotism.

When the Declaration of Independence was signed, the words "all men are created equal" were conditional, but it was an ideal that we could move towards as a nation. It was a belief that many referred to in that document and others as being emblematic as what America stands for and what we should work towards. It can be argued that this is the ideal that is representative, despite its faults, that people see in the American flag. There is no flag of the Confederacy which can boast that same heritage and honor as bestowed upon it when looking upon the foundation of the Confederate government as being expressly created for the means of maintaining white supremacy and chattel slavery.

The narrative of "Pride, Heritage, and Honor" is further complicated when we look at things like the resurgence of the "Stars and Bars" during the 1950s en masse in response to social changes that the south was not on board with and the official adoption of the emblems onto state flags across the south to further show their displeasure with the changing tide. When one argues that the flag they are flying is about history or heritage, it calls into question what heritage and history they are trying to embrace. Are they longing for a time in which they were rebellious to the Union and sought open armed conflict or are they honoring the period in which this flag was omnipresent to remind blacks of their place in society despite any court rulings or support from the Federal government to enforce the law?

Heritage is a vague term and a very cozy one to offer up when you want someone to accept your version of the story. It lacks details, information, clarity, and can ultimately omit the truth. The truth about heritage is that it is a lie. It is a bold face lie to make people comfortable with avoiding the past. It makes every bad thing that is associated with that flag an ignored reality. The words pride and heritage would no longer carry weight in any discussion encompassing the Confederate flag. The words pride and heritage should not have enough power to remove the deep, scarring imprint that this flag and those who committed horrible misdeeds while aligned to it created. It is worn as a badge of honor when it is a source of shame.

The Pride and Heritage arguments are much like a Fun House mirror in that they provide a distorted image or reality. The unsettling truth about Fun House mirrors is that when you walk away, you have to face the reality that the image you have been peering into does not exist. The image presented is not the only distortion.

The fabrication and false truth that many keep telling themselves is comfortable and they are complacent enough that they do not believe the true image they are faced with when they are, in fact, given evidence of the reality. The aspects of which so much pride is invested is a complete farce. It is Margaret Mitchell fan fiction erotica. When this false image and distorted past are torn down, the only resort is to try to recreate that history and make excuses for it in some way. There is a need to change the narrative and try to pull people back into the fun house with you. It is where you were comfortable. It is where you were safe. It is where this identity was real.

The reality is that true Southern Pride could be seen in the actions of those who resisted the hatred of their neighbors. It could be seen in the residents of Jones County, Mississippi through seceding from the Confederacy. It could be seen in those who decided to stay in the south despite the Jim Crow legislation and the constant denigration of them. Their pride and dignity could not be robbed of them. It is not something that any of us could imagine. These are circumstances that none of us would want to assume and trade our lives for in order to even gain a glimpse of just for the mere experience.

The pride in their humanity and the reality that they mattered and wanted to create a reality for their children in which they would be able to look someone of the other race in the eye when talking to them and not have it seen as threatening, for their children to attend schools that were not falling apart, to buy a home and live where they pleased and exercise the ideals and philosophies that are spelled out in the founding documents that helped shape this nation.

Their pride and dignity holds much more weight than that of the pride that many would argue is held within a flag that is linked to the power structures who helped to keep them as second-class citizens. When they see this flag, it is not with a sense of pride, it is a reminder of a past that they do not want any part of nor want to return to. It is a reminder of a world in which their opinions, rights, and humanity do not matter. Knowing that my grandparents were able to survive through this period gives me great pride in them. Knowing that there were so many of their generation who were willing to cut a path in order to ensure many of us would be able to have the freedoms, rights, and level of equality recognized by society, makes me grateful for their place in history.

There is much more to be proud of when thinking about the countless individuals who struck out against the injustices played out on them. True pride is seen in their actions and the legacy that they laid out for the following generations. There is not much pride, honor, or dignity in standing as an obstacle to an entire race, culture, or demographic of people seeking to attain democratic representation and the same rights and freedoms that others have had, exercised, and enjoyed for generations. It is the ultimate hypocrisy. To claim that there is pride or honor in these deeds runs counter to what the ideals of what America and the American dream is supposed to embody. It is far from patriotic. One should be willing to stand up for another's rights and ensuring that they are part of the American framework.

The banner being waved throughout the south should not be met with measures of pride, but should be admonished and open to ridicule. It should be seen as a badge of shame instead of honor. The banners were not waved out of pride. They were waved in defiance of social progress. They were brought into the public space in order to demonstrate their disregard for federal laws and the disagreement with regulations requiring them to recognize that their black neighbors were now on equal footing as them. Equality would change the narrative that "everything was fine as long as you weren't a nigger." With them being on equal footing, what would that mean for the average person in the south? The only choice was to remind these black people of all backgrounds of who was superior. Southern whites began to unfurl the "Southern Cross" in the path of progress which became a universal and accepted sign that read "unwelcome."

The reality is that the heritage they revere is much closer to that of *Uncle Tom's Cabin, Incidents in the Life of A Slave Girl, Running A Thousand Miles For Freedom,* and *Our Nig* rather than the version chronicled in the pages of *Gone with the Wind*. It is not this romanticized identity. It is not this view of themselves as the victor and the victim all at once.

Breaking from the myth means that they have to come to terms with acknowledging that they have not only been lying to themselves, but to the entire world for generations. In turn, they have been victims of this myth. It is devastating to have to deal with this and no wonder that someone would want to cling to this piece of fabric and present it the world as a testament of their glory and defiance to oppression.

To comes to terms with this means that they have to admit that flag and what it represents is an amalgamation of Simon Legree, Nathan Bedford Forrest, George Wallace, "Dynamite" Bob Chambliss, and everything that helps to stagnate social progress. Southern Heritage is so much more than this. It is Sweet Tea (not that garbage that chain restaurants serve and try to pretend is sweet tea), Jack Daniels,

Crawfish etouffé, Coca-Cola, SEC Football (The only college football worth watching), NASCAR, biscuits and gravy, barbecue, making fun of the neighboring state, having more churches and dirt roads per capita than any other part of the country, and so many other defining characteristics that make up the culture of the region and its people.

There is much more that helps to define a people and a history than the revised history associated with a piece of cloth. I would much rather argue over a gumbo recipe (anything from Houston is terrible) and debate the finer points of why the SEC, even when they don't win the National Championship, is still the best college football conference.

I was born in the south and raised there for the majority of my life. The Confederate Battle flag is the last thing that I considered to being equivalent to Southern heritage, pride, or honor. It didn't tell my story or the countless stories of many of those who had lived in the South for generations.

We must reserve and understand that this narrative of honor, pride, and heritage is much profound and has a deeper meaning and impact.

When considering the obstacles that many

people had to overcome in response to those individuals who were oftentimes waving these flags, these symbols in order to signify that they were not welcome, they were not equal, they were not worthy of sharing the same spaces, having the same rights, exercising the same freedoms, the people who stood up to those "defenders" of the "Southern way of life" carved out a path for all of us and are the true embodiment of Southern Pride, Heritage, and Honor.

That flag and what it truly represents was and is the antithesis of these principles and ideals of Pride, Heritage, and Honor. That flag means nothing to me.

"I am not your Magical Negro"

Education had always been my personal passion both in pursuit and profession. I felt as though one should always better themselves through the pursuit of knowledge, focus on critical thinking, and always strive to become more. After I completed my first degree, I was at the crossroads of what to do. For a short period, I considered pursuing a career in education and entered the program at my school to become certified.

As part of the process, there are a number of courses that you must take discussing the methodologies of education, curriculum, psychology, etc. One of the first classes that I was registered for was Special education, as required by the program. The course covered all aspects of the issue including legal cases and ways to include students of all abilities. There was even a redefining of the term for many in that room. It did not include many with afflictions and disabilities, but also those who were labeled as gifted.

My mood soured about education and the course when we were introduced to a guest speaker who visited to discuss her program and how it may affect educators. Despite all that she had to say, there was only one thing that stood out to me during her presentation. She discussed numerous students and provided a video of their abilities backing up why they were labeled as gifted. Student after student on display had their skills in science and math or even public speaking demonstrated.

One of my friends, Stan, joked with me while we were watching the video that there were only white kids in the gifted program. He whispered to me, "Oh. Only white folks get to be in these classes? What? Black people aren't good enough?"

When he made his comment a couple of students gave him a look as though he had broken some social norm or was somehow offensive in making the comment, especially with it coming out of a white mouth.

I just looked at him, gave him a nod, confirming his suspicions.

He and I met working at the local movie theater when I first started college and he stated to me from time to time that he, being a progressive white guy, definitely was a fish out of water having moved from the Northeast to go to college in this rural Georgia town as he saw the interactions, and lack thereof, between the black and white residents and college students.

As the presenter continued, I saw what I started to fear. She had a "Token Black" kid in her gifted program. I laughed internally and tried to keep control of my facial expressions. After the dozen or so students that she had discussed at length, she introduced this one. The way that she made him a part of the class and on display for the gifted program did not sit well with me. After demonstrating all the academic strengths of all of the other students, valid reasons as to why they are in the gifted program, and lauding over their accomplishments, she shows a video of him at a talent show doing an impression of Michael Jackson, complete with the sequined glove and moonwalk. She continued to rave about his dancing ability and how well he impersonated "MJ."

There was nothing reflecting his intellectual ability or his academic skills. There was nothing to demonstrate to us, people who were training to enter the field of education, that we should take these students' accomplishments seriously or praise them in the same light as their peers. There was nothing about this display that demonstrated inclusiveness or his role in the program. This video did nothing more than to showcase his ability for an impersonation.

As I looked around as she was playing the video, no one else seemed to understand this contradiction, this problem with the situation, except for Stan. I looked over and asked him if he noticed at all how odd this was. This entire room of future educators did not see how this educational leader had failed to demonstrate this student's academic abilities. She displayed his performance talents which would not be a problem if everyone else on display had their talents and abilities showcased, but this was the only thing that was on display for this young man and it created a juxtaposition between himself and the several other students that were shown to the class. It did nothing to allow these education students to see him for his academic abilities and strengths. He was simply on display for entertainment. This unfortunately would allow for these individuals to carry this perspective about their students into their own respective careers.

Several years later, I found myself with the opportunity to teach in Suburban Phoenix once I left the Army. Fortunately, I was offered a position to teach US history and Civics for Juniors and Seniors in 2009.

The opportunity afforded me the ability to instruct students on the cusp of exiting High school and entering college. They were at the end of their adolescence and entering adulthood. This is one of the ideal times to meet with students, mentor, effect change, and have a vital impact on their lives. I was ready to begin teaching once the ink met the paper on my contract for that upcoming year.

I was off to a great start. I sponsored a few clubs, mentored students, volunteered as a chaperone for several events, and looked for any possible way to connect with my students. Much to my delight, word had gotten back to the principal about the impact that I was having. Several parents had contacted him about how their children were now approaching education with a new outlook and had more interest in topics that, on the surface, seemed anything but interesting or entertaining.

After the first year, the principal recommended that I join the Advancement Via Individual Determination (AVID) program to help encourage students to pursue their college education. At first, I was excited about participating in such a program that afforded me the ability to offer my insight into college and career paths as part of the program and to help guide many of these students on their course. Unfortunately, after the first year, I was finding it very difficult to do my job as a result of the constant meddling of the assistant principal. After much thought and consideration, I decided to schedule a meeting with her to remove myself from the program and return to solely teaching history courses.

As I waited for our meeting, I considered all of the options in front of me that day. For weeks, I had thought about the decision I was about to make and how much it may affect me and my future employment. Some administrators are understanding, while others want you to "play ball." I was tired. I was frustrated with doing what was asked of me and more in order to teach my students only to receive criticism after criticism for helping them learn more, expand their reading, prepare for college, and mentor them throughout the past two years. This program wasn't the problem. The interference from the assistant principal and the lack of support along the way was.

I met with the assistant principal that morning to discuss the program with the full intention of explaining my future, or lack thereof, with it. As I entered her office, I thought about the words that would come out of my mouth. She took a seat behind her desk and asked, "What can I help you with?"

"Well, I wanted to let you know that I would like to leave the AVID program and return to teaching solely history courses as per my initial hiring." The look on her face was of pure bewilderment.

"I'm kind of shocked that you would want to stop teaching in the program. You've been doing very well and I have enjoyed having you as a part of it."

I had to bite my tongue. Her words were overshadowed by her actions over the past year. She repeatedly questioned my style and undermined the way that I taught whenever visiting my room. I had to cater my response so I did not cause a stir.

"I would prefer to return to teaching the Government and US History courses that I was hired to teach."

"I have to admit that I am a little disappointed. We may not have a full-time position available for you if you only want to teach history. Are you sure that is what you want?"

In my head, I knew this was ridiculous. The school was expanding its enrollment and has never had a problem filling classes. Many of them were at or beyond capacity as it was. It also made me even more confident in what I was planning as she seemed to be basing my future employment on whether or not I would back down on this issue.

"Yes. I would much rather prefer teaching history. It is my field."

"I have to say that this is comes truly as a surprise to me and I really don't want to lose you in the program. We really need a teacher of color."

Come again?

I thought as though I had broken from reality in that moment when she made that comment. Not only was it unprofessional, but highly inappropriate. She had referred to me as "a teacher of color." There was no reference to needing me because of my professionalism, work ethic, credentials, or experience. She invoked race. I wasn't even sure how to respond. My intentions when I first met with her were to address my desire to change my instructional schedule, however, she completely changed the framework of this entire meeting by bringing up my race as the reason I should stay on as a member of the school college readiness program. Why was bringing up race necessary? How did this even pertain to our meeting? I asked for clarification and her response took us even deeper into her vortex.

"What do you mean?"

"Well, you are the only teacher of color we have in the program and you are so good with the black and Hispanic students. We really need *you*."

I thought to myself again at how absurd this all was. I was teaching for a school whose attendance was roughly 4500 students with 180 faculty members, 6 of whom were black. Of those, I was the only black male curriculum teacher. The others taught vocational or elective courses. In the 15-year history of the school, I was just the second curriculum teacher who happened to be a black male and only the 7th total that the school had employed. I understood the basics of what she was trying to convey. She may have meant to complement me on mentoring my students and being a role model to them. The problem was her approach and the way that she did it. There was no place for this in the conversation that we were conducting. Additionally, like many educators, she made the mistake of assuming that the only way to reach out to your black and brown students is by having a black or brown face in front of them. By this logic, none of the minority population had been served, or was at least underserved, before I had arrived. Somehow, they were not receiving any outreach or the teachers that were there somehow did not teach them the same as their white students, according to her line of reasoning. In the same respect, one would make the assumption that I could not reach out to and achieve the same results with my white and Asian students. I found this whole situation absurd.

The problem and perspective was wholly ingrained, at least with some of the schools where I worked and particularly through the way that educators and administration would handle educational programs, as well as, discipline. One particular incident, in the same school, occurred during a faculty meeting. All members congregated in the auditorium for a variety of issues that the district and the school administration had arranged for us to cover. As the meeting rolled along the topic turned to Advanced Placement (AP) courses and test scores. The principal wanted to discuss the findings of the most recent assessments and the demographics of our programs in comparison to the state and national averages. As the slides progressed, he made special note of those that reflected the low number of Hispanic and black students enrolled in the AP programs.

"We really need to get more Black and Hispanic kids enrolled."

He pointed out the issue but not a way to address it. There was no discussion about approaching students, engaging them, or even about the benefits of the advanced placement program. There was a great opportunity for these educators, if they truly wanted to advocate change in their field to be given direction and ideas of how to lead and recruit a more diverse student body into the AP program. Doing so would put many of the students on much more solid academic footing. Unfortunately, the conversation moved on. The next slide in his presentation featured the test results for the program.

"As you can see... here are the results for AP History... Science... and Math...We tested higher than the state in all of these categories and highest in math out of all three."

There was some clapping and some light congratulations that ensued in the room and after a pause with a little self-reflection the Principal then stated something that didn't need to be said nor shouldn't have been said during this meeting.

"Thank God for all those Asian kids!"

A chorus of laughs echoed throughout the auditorium. Thankfully they covered up my response to his statement of "Are you fucking kidding me?"

As I walked out of that meeting I came face to face with all of the championship banners for sports and numerous athletic accolades the school had acquired in its short history. It all became quite clear from that moment. The faculty, administration and even the support system was more focused on recruiting black and brown kids into the athletics programs and paid lip service to their participation in the academic ones. There was no real emphasis placed on getting these kids in more rigorous academic programs. The problem that they suffered from was deeper than wanting and needing another teacher of color.

Fit to be Tied

Can I just wear a bow tie in peace? It seems like a minor request, something that seems so inconsequential, but if there is one piece of attire that has caused more heads to turn and more stares to appear on people's faces as I walk by it is a bowtie. Strange comments and conversations have occurred simply because, at times, I choose this accessory.

I would get it if I were wearing an ascot or bolo tie, but even then, I think the response would pale in comparison to that when people see me wearing the "Instant Black Muslim" costume. I'm greeted with *A salaam alaikum* or asked my thoughts on Malcolm X. White people who wear bowties become "geeks," academic administrators, scholars, or conservative political pundits while black folk automatically become members of the Nation of Islam.

NIGGER

The usage of the word "Nigger" creates much tension, anger, and confusion between blacks and whites. The question comes up as to who is permitted to use it and it what context is it permissible. Is there an actual "pass" given with respect to using the term? Additionally, is there a difference with the type of "N-Word" that one is using? Is there a distinction between Nigger, Nigga, Nigguh, Nigra, Nig, or any other derivative that may at some date and place appear? In short, no. The difference, for the most part comes down to intent. What is meant by your use of the word? Is it a way to gain acceptance within the black community? If that is the case, there are so many other ways to accomplish this that do not involve using such racially charged language, even if it is meant in an attempt to create some sort of bond. Why the hell do you want to say it anyway?

The popularity of black culture in movies, film, and television has pushed the availability and accessibility of this word throughout mainstream America in a way that has become all too confusing for many people.

Often, I have been confronted with the position that if black people can use the taboo N-

Word, then why can't white people? It is true that with some black people the N-Word, and its offshoots, is and can be used as a term of endearment amongst one another. The problem is that one cannot cross that line of being on the outside and using that same term to refer to any of your black friends or you will quickly be corrected for your error. You might not like the response or correction to your lapse in judgment. Your motivations in usage will be questioned. Your racial prejudices may even be exposed. Besides, not all black people use the term or accept its use. It is a term that many of us do not use or tolerate even in ordinary interactions with friends and family.

This may seem a little confusing to many people who do not feel as though they are at all racist or have ever had a racist thought in their minds, however, when you have challenged this social norm, it is hard to rectify yourself with your friends on the matter, even if they say otherwise. Our minds will register doubts that will persist throughout the remainder of our relationship. No matter the level or length of the friendship and association, there is little that can be done to heal this injury. *We're cool, but we ain't that fucking cool.* The moment the words comes out of your mouth, we begin to question the trust that we have had in you for the duration that we have been acquainted. We consider and question why this word is being used. We ponder how long you may have considered using this in the past and whether or not you see me in this way. *Am I just a nigger to you?*

One of the first moments when I was confronted with this reality took place in High School. A friend of mine and I were sitting in English class goofing off about some piece of reading our teacher gave us at the time. Being that it was Senior English and only one semester to go before graduation, many of us had little thought about taking too many things seriously. We had a case of full blown "senioritis."

Out of nowhere, "nigger" pops out of my friend's mouth, and it is directed at me. It wasn't a nigga, nigguh, or even a figment of my imagination. When I confronted him about his statement, he immediately became defensive.

"Man, I was just playing with you. You say 'whiteboy this, whiteboy that' all the time."

I looked at him dejected and puzzled. This was complete bullshit. The word "whiteboy" had not come out of my mouth nor was it something that I referred to him as. I was even more frustrated that he was trying to somehow validate the offense he had committed in deflecting it with a fabrication of events in which I was somehow the aggressor.

My blood boiled. My head started to throb. *Who the fuck is this guy? I'm a nigger? That's what I am in his eyes. That's all that I am. That's what he sees me as and felt comfortable enough to try and excuse it. We had the same courses over the years, played ball together, and even stayed over at each other's houses, but to this motherfucker, I'm just a nigger.*

I knew how it would play out. If I were to get angry over this and cause a scene or worse, get into a fight over it, the end result would be nothing more than me coming out the worse for it. I stood up and grabbed my books to take a seat on the opposite side of the room.

"Dude, the fuck is wrong with you?"

Somehow, I was the problem.

"I refuse to sit next to someone who is content in calling me 'Nigger' as if it were my name. Besides, I thought that you would be more comfortable having some space between you and a 'Nigger.'"

"You're overreacting."

Overreacting?!?!?

I gritted my teeth.

"Go… fuck… yourself."

I clenched my fist. I wanted to hit him. I wanted to drive my fist through his face and knock him to the ground. I wanted him to physically feel the pain that I was feeling emotionally. Again, I thought about what the end result would be. I would not win through any type of physical reaction no matter how badly I wanted it or how justified I would feel in doing so.

I looked over at the other side of the room and began walking to the only vacant seat. Distance is what I needed. Space. Another group of people I had come to know over the years were sitting there. From the look on my face and demeanor when I sat down, they knew something was up and asked me what had happened. Reluctantly, I let them in on the recent incident. They were a bit taken aback that this was said and one of them even commented that I should have kicked his ass for saying something like that.

As angry and frustrated as I was at the time, my focus was on the fact that this is a concept that people cannot begin to fathom. It was more than just about him saying it. It was about the dehumanization of someone through that word. The intention was nowhere near permissible.

Today, the argument often becomes one of who has ownership of the word and who has the right to say it. People even ask whether or not someone should be offended at being called this word when black people do it daily in conversations, music lyrics, comedic performances, and film. Despite this, it still does not give someone license, no matter their level of familiarity the right or privilege to use the word with an individual of color.

The trust and bond between white and black friends becomes frayed at this point because we cannot see our white friends as free from prejudice, racial bias, or bigotry anymore. The line has been crossed. The action cannot be undone nor can we be reassured that this is not the way that you view other people of color or us when committing this infraction.

I was proven correct in my feelings about the situation when later that year, the school district received a new superintendent of instruction. He had a life-long career in education, a PhD, and numerous accolades. He wasn't some guy the district hired off of the street in order to add more color to appear more diverse and inclusive.

Despite it being a racially diverse school population, I had only one teacher of color in the years I had gone to school in Georgia and she was a substitute. As part of the new superintendent's mission statement, he encouraged more rigorous classes and content.

One of the first changes that he made was to eliminate final exam exemptions for students thus requiring them for all including those with "A" averages, which had been the previous practice. This sent a number of students and teachers into a panic by having to conform to the new changes. One of these individuals most upset was my "friend."

One of the courses we shared was Journalism, which afforded us the freedom to work in the computer lab before school and during lunch. At the time, several of us were working on our articles and columns for the paper, including one student whose assignment was composing a feature on the new superintendent. All of a sudden, the door swings open and my "friend" charges into the room while in the midst of a tirade.

"I was all ready to have the last week of school off, and this FUCKING NIGGER had to come along and ruin it!"

He gave little consideration as to who was there to serve as an audience to this performance. There were three people in that room when he barged in. He was only aware of two, not noticing that I was part of the trio. The two girls I had been working alongside sat there dumbfounded at what he said. As he continued berating this man that he never met, he noticed I was seated five feet from him and began backpedaling.

It was too late. He had confirmed the suspicions I had of him since he had called me that same racial slur just months prior. It was something that many black friends and coworkers think when someone around them "slips" and uses that word. *What was the intent? Is there something malicious here? Is it something out of a temporary lapse in judgment?* We all have moments where words spill from our mouths due to anger and do not take the time to think about what we are saying, but there was time to form what was coming out of his mind and transfer that message to the other two in the room who he thought would be receptive to what he had to say. He thought this man was a Nigger, and he meant it. When he referred to me as the same, there was no confusion. This idea that he would see any of us as equals was inexistent. He only saw us as one thing; Niggers.

We were the class of '96. One with much promise and potential. I had long been told that racism and ignorance would die out as those older white racists died out. What never gets mentioned or even considered when I hear people repeat this line is that bigots have kids too. They bring up their kids with many of the same beliefs and do not break the mindset of racial superiority. It is taught and cultivated. It festers and grows.

The same incidents and conversations I was having 20 years ago, I am still witnessing today. We can't collectively wait for racists and bigots to die or hope that they change their mindset on their own.

Their actions, attitudes, and behaviors have effects that reach deeper than their immediate company.

I lost count over the years as to how many times and ways in which I have been called the "N-Word," or had it stated in my presence. I have born witness to as it would come out of the mouths of professors, employers, customers, friends, co-workers, colleagues, students, and strangers.

It is not something where a simple apology remedies the injury. There is history, a sordid, dark history with this word and its application. It is not a mark that can disappear in an instant. It is a stain that remains in perpetuity on the individual saying it and the person whom it is directed.

Nearly 15 years had passed in which I found myself clear across the country. I was in the midst of a relationship with a young lady I had met while I was living in Atlanta, GA. This courtship was not free of its moment of confronting the N-Word. Jennifer and I had been dating for 8 months, most of which had been consumed by my military training while I was stationed at Fort Benning. We visited each other when time permitted in order to achieve some sense of a normal relationship. When I had finished one period of training, I flew out to Arizona in order to spend some time with her. She grew up there and had just moved back from Atlanta after being offered a new job in the Phoenix area. I was truly interested in getting to see Arizona and meet her family while I was there. My experience and knowledge of the southwest was limited to my father's affinity for westerns.

The weekend I visited coincided with the birthday of her grandmother. Several of her relatives would be in attendance for her dinner. I was concerned with making the right impression. As we rode to the restaurant, she played an assortment of hip-pop (the commercial garbage that was usually played on the radio and fell short of the authenticity expressed in real hip-hop) and sang along. I found it a bit annoying in that the time I had known her, anything black was a novelty to her.

She saw the "cool" side of black culture and embraced it in the same way that many white suburban kids did. It was exotic. It was the forbidden fruit that gave them the opportunity to live what they viewed as black culture vicariously. There was little to no proximity for them so they had to settle for music, TV, movies, comedians, and athletes in order to get a sense of the identity and circumstances surrounding blackness. They are able to partake in the culture and people without being taken out of their comfort zones. Jennifer was the embodiment of this. She loved hip hop and R&B, Tyler Perry movies, and pretty much anything and everything deemed "ethnic."

She would recount to me the times that she would prefer going to parties thrown by the black fraternities at the University of Arizona because they had better music and she felt she would have a better time. I classified her as a Negrophile or even as a quasi-Negroologist, in that she wanted to absorb anything about the culture, on the surface, but there was nothing about the depth that she was willing to learn.

To her, black culture and history was Diddy, Beyoncé, and Jay-Z. She had no knowledge of the Harlem Renaissance, the Harlem Hellfighters, 54th Massachusetts, W.E.B. DuBois, Paper Bag Tests, The "Triple Nickels," Dorothy Dandridge, Songhai, Shaka Zulu, Mandela, Lumumba, Frantz Fanon, Jim Crow, the brutal murder of Emmett Till, the Watts Riots, the significance of James Meredith's enrollment at Ole Miss or Ruby Bridges' first day of school. There was a connection with the pop cultural elements, but a disconnect with the reality of the culture and history. Her understanding was superficial, but it was understandable considering she was raised in a state that was the last to adopt the Martin Luther King holiday.

She sat there in the driver's seat singing along to the playlist she had assembled. I braced myself. I knew the moment was approaching where this song would reach what I was anticipating. I felt a little black version of Paul Revere tap me on my shoulder.

The Niggers are coming!!! The Niggers are coming!!!

I knew that lyrics littered with the N-Word were on the horizon. The one thing I wanted to see was whether or not she was going to sing along or play it off.

Then it happened. I sat there in the car and heard the words "all the niggas and bitches in the club..." come out of her mouth. Without any hesitation, I reached over and turned the stereo off.

"What the hell did you just say?"

The response was just as oblivious as her action. "Huh?"

"Niggas? You just said niggas over and over."

"So??? I was just singing along with the song."

"You can't just start singing 'niggas' because it's in the song. You can't use that as an excuse. You better hum that part, substitute some other words, or sing it in your head."

"What do you mean I can't say nigga?"

What do you mean you can't say nigga?

As I looked at her, I could see the wheels turning. She was becoming overcome with confusion: *I have a black boyfriend… I had a black friend in middle school… I'm not racist… I like rap music… I love Beyoncé…*

That is where the problem resides. Palate does not determine association, identification, or inclusion to an experience and history. There is the misunderstanding that a loose connection with black culture creates an air of familiarity for some people. There is this misconception that because one has black friends, a black spouse, black relatives, or even voted for Barack Obama, that they are afforded a "pass" when it comes to micro-aggressions and missteps.

The trust and bond has been broken between people. At that point, trust cannot be reestablished. There is no sense of shared identity with that word or shared history with that pain. Even if I were someone who were to use it in my personal life and amongst my friends, it is not something that if, as serving as a "gatekeeper," someone on the outside could fully fathom when they were called this word out of anger, friendship, endearment, trust, etc. There is a lack of identity with the word that those on the outside have and cannot appreciate which causes this rift with being able to use it. It is not simply an issue of using the word, because, let's be frank, no one needs anyone's permission to use any one word.

When this subject has come up in the past, as it will more than likely come up in the future, many people reference the use of the N-Word by black people. I am here to tell you that this is a generalization that has made it into the mainstream that many people have accepted as a social norm, a fact, and a reality. They have used this as a way to justify their possible use of this same word. There are people who use the N-word as a term of endearment amongst their peers. We witness its use in popular music and movies. We do not have it occur in daily interactions and professional settings with people. There are many black people who despise the use of the word "Nigger" in all its forms. They want to have it removed from the public dialogue. There have been mock funerals for the word by social organizations throughout the nation several times to emphasize the importance of removing this word and the tarnished legacy that it has left on African-Americans and the image that it has presented to the rest of America.

Regardless of this, there are people who want access to the "club" in the ability to say "Nigger" or "Nigga" any time and in any circumstances.

I ran across this when teaching in Arizona. The school's demographics were "ethnically challenged."

This led to some interesting conversations in our Social Studies discussion circles. The topic of race came up more than a few times because my students felt the need to ask me questions, being that I was the only black teacher that they had had, not just in high school, but ever in some cases. There was a nearby school where they were considering removing Mark Twain's classic novel "Huckleberry Finn" because of the use of "Nigger" strewn throughout. A student complained to the school about the language in the book and his parents appealed to have the book removed. This led to our debate topic for that day as to discussing literary freedom. As we got deeper into that discussion, some of the students revealed their music choices which have the same amount of use of the N-Word, if not more. A few of them discussed how when they were with their black friends, they were "allowed" to use the N-Word. I wasn't at all surprised at this, nor was I surprised by the answer to my follow up question. I asked them if they only said it around their friends to which they replied "yes." I asked them why they don't say it in school or public or anywhere else. I pointed out to them that if their friends gave them permission to use the N-Word it should be fine, right? It was then that they in their discussion groups realized how the "arrangement" with their friends didn't make sense. They had an "in" with their friend for that moment and some sense of belonging because of the ability to do something that no one else could do. They had an advantage over many of their white peers who didn't share the same black friends or acquaintances. This gave them access. That is all it does, though. When I asked about using that word in public, there was an understanding that there was weight, history, and consequences behind the word even when I offered my personal "permission" to use it. There was still reluctance. When I asked why, the students responded that they didn't know how I would react if they said it.

They were right, that is the issue with the use of the word. Even when people make the false claim about a double-standard with the use of the word in stating that black people somehow have permission to use the word while white people do not, they admit that there is some problematic tortured history associated with the term. Despite the generalizations and misconceptions that are perceived and accepted, the majority of black people don't run around yelling "nigga this" and "nigga that" nor are they going to tolerate being talked to that way. It may be part of pop culture, but that is something more reserved in the realm of artistic license. Unfortunately, the reach of these forms of media allow for this viewpoint that an inordinate amount of the black community uses forms of the N-Word as filler within conversation. Oftentimes, those making this claim that there is some double standard and that black people are allowed to use this word while others are somehow deprived is a falsehood. One cannot pretend to be ignorant to this history in order to afford themselves the ability to use the word. There is no connection that can be made. Once you are honest and removed from the ignorance associated with the word, your desire to use the word or even bring up fallacious arguments like "double-standards" will disappear.

It is a complicated word with a dark history. It is a despicable, hateful, vile word that some have minimized to a term of endearment or even to one in which it can be tossed around as a common greeting. Despite the "romanticization" of the word, "Nigger" in its many forms carries an immeasurable amount of baggage.

Ignorance is never an acceptable excuse with regard to usage of the "N-Word." Many people fall back on the excuse of ignorance as a copout, a way to distance themselves from the offensive misstep. *I didn't know so there is no way they can find me at fault.* This would be valid if you were visiting America for the first time from some far-off land and had limited exposure to Americans and American culture. It might be understandable, but I was proven wrong on that front during a trip to Ures de Guadalupe, Mexico. One of my wife's relatives is affectionately known as "La Negra," which translates into English as "the Black." She earned this nickname as a child for being a shade or two darker than some of her cousins. Forty years later, she is still called by this rather than her actual name. During a conversation in which I was asking her a question, someone chimed in "you can't say that." I was curious. My Spanish is pretty bad, but I try to learn all of the bad stuff before anything else so I don't end up putting my foot in my mouth by offending anyone.

"Say what?"

"You can't say la Negra."

I was curious because for the years that I had known this woman, I had only heard her called, affectionately, by her nickname.

"What do you mean?"

In a thick accent, her cousin responded, "That's a really bad thing to say in English."

"But it just means black, right?"

"No... No... we don't call her that anymore because of what it means in America."

I was dumbfounded. "You can't call her 'black?' I thought that was her nickname."

My father-in-law, a man who had lived the vast majority of his life in Hermosillo and Bahia de Kino, Mexico, overheard the conversation, walked over and corrected her. "No, it's not the same. You can't say 'nigger.' That is really bad to say. It's racist."

I had to do a double-take. I'm in Ures, Mexico engaging in a discussion on the N-Word. The input on the part of "La Negra's" cousins was out of confusion over the similarities of the two terms, yet they did not excuse anyone's usage, even when they thought that I was saying it. They knew that the word was wrong to say and made the effort to ensure that others knew it, as well.

When someone argues that they want to use that word. My question to them is "Why do you want to use it? What compels you to want to call me or anyone else this?" What is it about this word that is driving you to use it?" James Baldwin once stated that the word "Nigger could start a fight or lead to a wedding." And that "the world is full of people who better not call him Nigger." (Baldwin, 1974) It is that complex. I don't wish to be referred to the N-Word in any form. It is not my name; it is in no way how I see myself or want to be seen. It is not how I have ever identified myself nor ever will.

There are no words to fully describe what it feels like to be dehumanized by being called this slur.

You are minimized and denigrated. Yet, when explaining this, people who don't want to accept the reality of the harm this word does try to simplify the situation to name calling. It trivializes the experience and history of the words and actions associated with the term. The best example I have ever encountered would come in the form of the poem "Incident" by Countee Cullen.

> Once riding in old Baltimore,
> Heart-filled, head-filled with glee,
> I saw a Baltimorean
> Keep looking straight at me.
>
> Now I was eight and very small,
> And he was no whit bigger,
> And so I smiled, but he poked out
> His tongue, and called me, 'Nigger.'
>
> I saw the whole of Baltimore
> From May until December;
> Of all the things that happened there
> That's all that I remember. (Cullen)

The deep scar left by this word is felt by multitudes of African-Americans. It is a term with a deep history and immeasurable weight. Instead of, when confronted, asking why you cannot say it, or feeling as though you are somehow a victim when people challenge you for using it, ask yourself why you even want to say it in any form. Why is it so important for you to be able to say "Nigger?"

Pride

"Why can't I be proud of being white?"

No one is saying that you can't be proud of your race or ethnicity, but there is a bit of confusion circulating around the black/white pride issue. The issue of pride related to being black comes on the heels of the civil rights movement and rebounding from the issues of the Jim Crow era which pushed many black people into the complacency of being ashamed of their identity or even a lack of knowledge with respect to their culture.

The issue and concept of being proud of their black identity is to respond to the decades of shame that had built into the mindset of black identity. The pride issue even turned into a movement where it became widespread to let not only black people in the south understand that they should have pride in themselves and who they are, but black people throughout the country. It was a united movement. It was about solidarity. It went beyond the borders of the United States and became an issue with black people in Europe, the Caribbean, and Africa to adopt the idea that their identity would not be wrapped around degradation and despair. The word and reality of pride as it is tied to one's identity reflects a rejection of all of the negative attitudes and stereotypes attributed to one's identity. Saying that one is proud of their heritage allows for an examination of all the ways that one is breaking free from the bondage of historical pain and negative circumstances and attributes that have been thrust upon them. They have had to carry this baggage and burden for generations.

When someone claims that they are perceived as racist when they state that are proud to be white, they are missing the point. There are no systemic or institutional prejudices placed on white identity allowing people to have negative perceptions about who they are as a white person and limit opportunities to them. There is no labeling of them as intellectually deprived, violent, uneducated, animalistic, lazy or prone to a life of crime and poverty as part of their culture. If someone wants to claim their white skin as a source of pride, there is no real issue. The only thing that they have overlooked is that if the only thing that they are proud of is their skin then that pride lacks any depth. "White" is the default setting for American identity. Many people, colors, and cultures are fighting for inclusion and against historical factors that have rendered them as being on the outside looking in.

If you are truly upset about not being able to say you're proud to be white without being thought of as a racist, think about those who prompted people to think about it in this way. It wasn't minorities or marginalized communities who made "White Pride" an issue of negativity. It was and is, people who want the term "White Pride" to signify being superior to non-whites. So, if you aren't racist and are actually anti-racism, take it up with those guys.

"WHY ARE BLACK PEOPLE SO ANGRY?"

We're not angry. We are passionate. There's a difference. Our words and sentiment can be intimidating, but do not be intimidated about it. Truthfully, we are tired of discussing race and issues of race, but we are more fatigued with being subject to racism. We are viewed as a collective monolithic entity rather than being seen as individual identities in society. Schools, businesses, the criminal justice system all place expectations, and for the most part, limitations on who we are. When we exceed in areas other than athletics, we are seen as cultural anomalies, outliers. When we get a good job or accepted to a "good school," Affirmative action is brought forth as the reason why we met with this success.

We are told to "not bring up the past" or "get over it" when discussing social, political, and historical issues when it is clear that the past and our histories played a prominent role win where we are today. We are tired of having the same conversation each time there is a denial of justice, racial profiling, or lack of equality. We are passionate about getting to a point where we have a true measure of equality instead of just on paper.

We are passionate about having our culture and history more accurately represented and included as part of the American fabric rather than being ridiculed for having 'our own month.' We are passionate about being more visible within the public space and having more of our stories told. Our passions are mistaken for anger. We want a piece of the American dream just like anyone else. To paraphrase Langston Hughes, we want to sit at the table and not be force to eat in the kitchen. When we do get a seat at the table we want more than "crumbs." We want to be visible. We want to be heard. We want our existence to have meaning.

We matter.

Bibliography:

Bill Cosby. 48 Vol. National Catholic Reporter, 2012. Print.

Tyler, Raymond. "Bill Cosby." *Philadelphia Weekly*: 52. 2006. Print.

Phillips, Joseph C. "Calling Out Bill Cosby." *Chicago Defender,* sec. XCIX: 14. 2005. Print.

Miller, Roy. "I Support Bill Cosby, but." *Westside Gazette,* sec. 33: 6. 2004. Print.

Price, Gilbert. "Bill Cosby's "Conservative" Message." *Call & Post,* sec. 91: 4A. 2007. Print.

Walker, Lee H. "Bill Cosby is Truly Free." *Chicago Independent Bulletin,* sec. 33: 9. 2004. Print.

Bonaparte, Kris. "Miscellaneous; Bill Cosby Said what!!!!!?" *Montreal Community Contact,* sec. 14: 25. 2004. Print.

Gee, Dana. "Education Opened the Door for Bill Cosby." *Calgary Herald*: C.16. 2013. Print.

Gruenwedel, Erik. "Bill Cosby Decries Slumping Urban Civility." *Video Store Magazine* 26.31 (2004): 16. Print.

Loeffler, William. "In the Beginning there was ... Bill Cosby." *McClatchy - Tribune Business News* 2010. Print.

Smith, Ryan E. "Bill Cosby Sticks with Comedy that Works." *McClatchy - Tribune Business News* 2010. Print.

Anonymous. "Bill Cosby: Sees Obamas as 'Huxtables'." *The Berkshire Eagle* 2008. Print.

Lopez, Robert C. "Expect Straight Talk from Bill Cosby." *McClatchy - Tribune Business News* 2008. Print.

"Bill Cosby: Let them Stay Mad." *The Jacksonville Free Press,* sec. 17: 15. 2004. Print.

Provost, Philip M. "Bill Cosby: On Laughs, Race and Pound Cake." *Arkansas Times* 38.30 (2012): 33. Print.

Rev Jesse Jackson. "We should Respect Bill Cosby's Contributions." *The Skanner,* sec. 28: 5. 2006. Print.

Anonymous. *Bill Cosby Blasts Hollywood's Portrayal of Blacks on Television.* 95 Vol. , 1999. Print.

Malveaux, Julianne. "Celebrating Dick Gregory." *Sun Reporter,* sec. 57: 1. 2000. Print.

Simmonds, Yussuf J. "Dick Gregory." *Sentinel,* sec. 72: A18. 2006. Print.

Joseph Omoremi. "Reparations Will Come: Dick Gregory." *Chicago Defender*: 5. 2000. Print.

Rahman, Ali. "A Conservation with Dick Gregory." *New York Amsterdam News*: 21. 2002. Print.

Chalmers, Robert. "Mr. Dick Gregory: Mr Incredible." *Chicago Weekend,* sec. 34: 5. 2005. Print.

"Dick Gregory Honored in Style." *Afro - American Red Star*: B1. 2000. Print.

Kirksey, Taaq. "Dick Gregory is Still Mr. Gregory." *Washington Informer*, sec. 42: 28. 2006. Print.

"Dick Gregory Returns to Chicago." *Chicago Independent Bulletin*, sec. 25: 14. 1996. Print.

Anonymous. *Dick Gregory Arrested in Embassy Protest*. 106 Vol. , 2004. Print.

Zaire, Gezus. "Dick Gregory Tells Columbus what's really Going on." *Call & Post*, sec. 92: 2A. 2008. Print.

Gregory, Dick. *Letters: Dick Gregory Defines Gangsta Rap*. 108 Vol. USA: Nielsen Business Media, 1996. Print.

Connors, Cathy. "Dick Gregory Visits Amsterdam News with Views." *New York Amsterdam News*, sec. 86: 34. 1995. Print.

Anonymous. "Dick Gregory: "Spike Lee is a Punk and a Thug."." *Chicago Citizen*, sec. 47: 12. 2013. Print.

Corey Manning. "Comedy is Only a Part of Legendary Activist Dick Gregory." *The Boston Banner*, sec. 46: 18. 2010. Print.

Robert Hurwitt. "Mort Sahl, Dick Gregory - Humor as Timely as Ever." *San Francisco Chronicle*: F.2. 2009. Print.

Krehbiel, Randy. "Dick Gregory Bringing His Frank Talk to Tulsa: NAACP Banquet." *McClatchy - Tribune Business News* 2007. Print.

"NAACP to Award 2004 Lifetime Achievement Award to Dick Gregory." *The Jacksonville Free Press,* sec. 18: 1. 2004. Print.

Lowe, Carlton. "You can be Anything You Want: A Night with Dick Gregory." *Washington Informer,* sec. 42: 28. 2006. Print.

Tate, Sonsyrea. "Long-Time Activist Thanks the Urban League: A One-on-One with Dick Gregory." *Washington Informer,* sec. 41: 20. 2005. Print.

Headlam, Bruce. "For Him, the Political has always been Comical." *New York Times (1923-Current file),* sec. 158: C1. 2009. Print.

Anonymous. *Gregory to Sue St. Louis Police for Violating His Rights and Fake Arrest.* 81 Vol. , 1992. Print.

Alexander, Kwame. *African American Humor: The Best Black Comedy from Slavery to Today.* 4 Vol. , 2002. Print.

Howard, Sherry L. "He's no Joke." *Emerge* 8.3 (1997): 46. Print.

Yourse, Robyn-Denise. "Gregory Looks for Hidden Agenda Behind Events." *New Pittsburgh Courier,* sec. 93: A1. 2002. Print.

Weide, Robert. "Whyaduck Productions, Inc. -- Dick Gregory: The Color of Funny."*Whyaduck Productions, Inc. -- Dick Gregory: The Color of Funny.* N.p., 12 Mar. 2012. Web. 1 Oct. 2013.

Akwamu, Kwasi. "Docl Gregory: All Jokes Aside." *The Michigan Citizen* 11 May 2002: n. pag. Print.

Cosby, Bill. "Bill Cosby Speech Transcript." *Bill Cosby Speech Transcript.* Rutgers University, n.d. Web. 28 Sept. 2013.

Bayliss, Deborah. "Activist Dick Gregory Delivers Wakeup Call to Blacks." *Chicago Weekend*: 2. Sept 1, 1996. Ethnic NewsWatch. Web. 29 Sept. 2013.

Baldwin, J. (1974). (J. Baldwin, Performer) University of California, Berkeley, Berkeley, California.

Obama, Barack. "A More Perfect Union -The Race Speech." Philadelphia, PA. 18 Mar. 2008.

"Countee Cullen." *Gale Literary Databases*. N.p., 2003.

The Token Black Guide

The Token Black Guide

ABOUT THE AUTHOR

Don Guillory is an historian, US Army Veteran, educator, and advocate for social justice. He is a graduate of Georgia Southern University, where he earned his Master of Arts in History, and Arizona State University where he earned his Master of Education. He currently teaches courses on history, race, and culture in Arizona where he lives with his wife and daughter.

Twitter: @donguillory

Email: TheTokenBlackGuide@gmail.com

Facebook: Token Black Guide

45814348R00155

Made in the USA
San Bernardino, CA
18 February 2017